$ 10.00

DEAN B. ELLIS LIBRARY

ACKNOWLEDGMENTS

I wish to express my gratitude to Secretary J. W. Crabtree and his associates at the headquarters of the National Education Association for their courtesy and helpfulness in making available certain materials needed in this study. I am under deepest obligation to Professor Daniel H. Kulp, II, under whose sponsorship the study has been made, for his thoroughgoing, detailed criticism, and to Professors David Snedden and Carter Alexander for their interest and advice at all stages of the undertaking.

E. S. S.

10/4/01

CONTENTS

CHAPTER	PAGE
INTRODUCTION	1
Purpose of Study	1
Method	1
Sociological Analysis: What It Is and What It Does	2
Objectives of the Study	5
Sources	6
Limitations	6
I. THE HISTORICAL BACKGROUND OF THE NATIONAL EDUCATION ASSOCIATION	9
Alexander's Study	9
The Period from 1910 to 1917	11
The Time Span of the Present Study, 1918 to 1928	13
II. EXPANSION IN MEMBERSHIP	14
Promotion Activities	15
Rivalry and Tradition as Factors in Expansion	20
Membership under Compulsion	22
Reorganization of the Association	23
Service to the Membership	24
The Campaign for a National Department of Education	25
Social Conditionings in the Situation	28
The Life Membership Plan	33
III. ORGANIZATION OF THE NATIONAL EDUCATION ASSOCIATION	35
The Representative Assembly	36
The Departments	44
The Executive Staff	48
Committees and Commissions	51
The National Council of Education	54
IV. THE ACTIVE RESPONSIBLE LEADERSHIP OF THE ASSOCIATION	57
Sex Distribution	59
Educational Positions of Leaders	60
Continuity of Service	62
Analysis of Leadership Data	66
Sex Distribution	66
Educational Positions of Leaders	68
Continuity of Service	70

Contents

CHAPTER	PAGE
V. ACTIVITIES AND OBJECTIVES OF THE ASSOCIATION	72
The Annual Convention	72
Addresses at General Sessions	72
Convention Resolutions	85
VI. ACTIVITIES AND OBJECTIVES (*Continued*)	94
Activities of the Executive Staff	94
Legislative Division	94
Division of Publications	98
The Bulletin	98
The Journal	99
Publicity	102
Proceedings	105
Other Publications	106
The Research Division	110
Division of Classroom Service	116
Division of Administrative Service	116
VII. ACTIVITIES AND OBJECTIVES (*Concluded*)	118
The Representative Assembly	118
Board of Directors	119
Executive Committee	121
Board of Trustees	123
VIII. CONFLICT AS AN ELEMENT IN THE ACTIVITY OF THE ASSOCIATION	128
Internal Conflict	129
External Conflict	133
IX. THE VARIETIES AND FORMS OF GROUP COÖPERATION	139
X. THE ASSOCIATION'S CONTROL OF ITS MEMBERS	148
XI. SUMMARY AND CONCLUSION	155
Expansion	155
Organization	156
Leadership	158
Activities	158
Conflict	161
Coöperation	161
Control	162
Problems Suggested by this Study	162
Conclusion: Practical Recommendations	164
SUPPLEMENT: THE ASSOCIATION AND THE WORLD WAR	167
APPENDIX	173
BIBLIOGRAPHY	177

TABLES

		PAGE
I.	Sex Distribution in Offices and in Leadership Subgroups of the National Education Association, 1918 to 1928, in Service-Years	59
II.	Sex Distribution in Offices of Departments of the National Education Association, 1918 to 1928	60
III.	Leaders of the Association, 1918 to 1928, Classified by Educational Position, in Service-Years	61
IV.	Members of Representative Assembly for 1926, 1927, and 1928, Classified by Educational Position and by Official Relationship to the Association	62
V.	Continuity of Service of State Directors of the National Education Association, 1918 to 1928	63
VI.	Continuity of Membership in the Representative Assembly of the National Education Association from Certain Selected States, 1924 to 1928	64
VII.	Continuity of Membership in Committees of the National Education Association, 1926 to 1928	66
VIII.	Addresses at General Sessions of the National Education Association Annual Conventions, 1918 to 1928, Classified under Defined Categories	73
IX.	A Complete Tabulation by Years and a Classification of Resolutions Adopted by the National Education Association at Its Annual Conventions, 1918 to 1928	86

CHART

A Graphic Representation of the Organization of the National Education Association 37

INTRODUCTION

PURPOSE OF STUDY

The purpose of this study is to subject the National Education Association of the United States to sociological analysis and interpretation in the following particulars: (1) its organization, (2) its leadership, (3) its activities and objectives, (4) its relationships to other groups, and (5) its methods of control. The period with which the study deals is from 1918 to 1928.

METHOD

A study of this kind obviously does not lend itself to experimental procedure. There can be no setting up of control conditions to test the efficiency of the present modes of functioning within the organization, as compared with other modes. Nor would a comparison of particular aspects of this group with the corresponding aspects of other voluntary associations now in existence yield significant results, because of the multiplicity of variant factors; factors such as size, sex distribution, age distribution, geographic distribution, tradition, economic status of members, societal status of the group, and its relationship to government. There are no abstract standards of composition or structure or size or functional efficiency by which an organization of this kind may be measured, and no comparative standards have been developed—perhaps none can be.

In any event, even if comparative studies were to be made and standards for teachers' associations were eventually to be determined, detailed studies of particular organizations would necessarily precede inter-group comparisons. Processes and functions and structures and relationships within a complex organization are themselves complex, and they must be subjected to intensive analysis in their own setting before they can be defined with sufficient accuracy to make possible their utilization in comparative studies and in the derivation of standards.

This, then, is a case study, an intensive sociological analysis or organic study of one complex group.

SOCIOLOGICAL ANALYSIS: WHAT IT IS AND WHAT IT DOES

A fundamental assumption in the application of the technique of sociological analysis to a "case"—that is, to a person or to a group or to a limited phase of personal or group life—is that there can be no valid understanding except as the object of study is viewed whole rather than piecemeal. It is to be viewed as an organic unit made up of complex, interrelated elements, not as an aggregate of distinct, unrelated elements. As Miss Palmer has said:

> The meaning of each factor is sought in terms of its relationship to other factors and in terms of its relationship to the results which are observed, for it is recognized that it is the study of factors as integral parts of different social situations, and not the study of these factors in isolation, that leads to the understanding of group behavior. It is from this very complete description of what actually happens that the investigator is able to extract the vital processes which make the group what it is, and from this analysis, in turn, to infer new canons that govern collective action.[1]

D. H. Kulp, II, in his *Country Life in South China,* pages xiv and xix, characterizes as follows studies that use the organic method:

> Intensive studies of selected groups, villages, or regions analyzed in detail and presented in an organic way so that the relationships and correlations of the facts discovered will disclose functions, processes, and trends. . . . A plan wherein all the details of a delimited culture group are studied in their natural conjunctions, relationships, and interdependencies.[2]

The attempt is made in the present study to apply the methods of organic sociological analysis to an organized, special-interest group. This should be considered as the first of a series of studies of the

---

[1] Palmer, Vivien, M., *Field Studies in Sociology,* p. 20.

[2] Cf. Thomas, W. I. and Znaniecki, F., *The Polish Peasant in Europe and America,* I, p. 10: "No . . . group of social facts can be treated theoretically and practically in an arbitrary isolation from the rest of the life of the given society."
See also:
Giddings, F. H., *The Scientific Study of Human Society,* Chap. VI (The Study of Cases).
Ellwood, C. A., "Recent Developments in Sociology," in *Recent Developments in the Social Sciences,* edited by E. C. Hayes, Chap. I.
Cooley, C. H., "The Life Study Method as Applied to Rural Social Research," *Publications of the American Sociological Society,* XXIII (1929), pp. 248-54.
Thomas, W. I., "The Behavior Pattern and the Situation," *Publications of the American Sociological Society,* XXII (1928), pp. 1-13.
It is interesting to note that this "organic" approach to a study of phenomena, as distinct from the atomistic approach, has gained acceptance in the physical and biological as well as in the social sciences. See, for example, A. N. Whitehead, *Science and the Modern World;* W. E. Ritter and Edna W. Bailey, *The Organismal Conception, Its Place in Science and Its Bearing on Philosophy;* and C. M. Child, "Biological Foundations of Social Integration," *Publications of the American Sociological Society,* XXII (1928), pp. 26-42.

Introduction 3

National Education Association, for it is not possible, within the scope of the present study, to make a complete sociological analysis of this immense group. Therefore, certain limitations of this investigation have been established, as will be indicated later.

A word should be said as to the use of quantitative techniques in case studies. Statistical and case-study methods are not to be thought of as opposed to each other, but rather as mutually supplementary. An investigation of the distribution of a trait, of a process, or of a kind of activity, if it is strictly limited to the fact of distribution, is obviously a purely statistical study. But in so far as such a study takes account of conjunctivities and sequences and of what may be called conditioning factors in a particular person or group or movement, to that extent it has the essential character of a case study. On the other hand, although "for the most part the data from case studies appear in the form of 'running accounts,' narratives of events, and descriptions of personalities and situations . . ., it is often convenient to present particular aspects of the case on charts or schedules"[3] and to summarize them in statistical form.

Moreover, in a study of "single situations, persons, groups, or institutions as complex wholes in order to identify types and processes," the investigator may be guided by the outcome of purely quantitative techniques in the choice of cases to be studied, in the selection of the particular aspects of a case to be investigated, and certainly in the determination of priority of investigation. The use of quantitative methods, far from being incompatible with the case-study method, is occasionally essential to it. Nevertheless, it is true that many fundamental phases of a case or organic study are non-quantitative—phases such as analyses of functional processes, for example. In these the data must be assembled and analyzed, the relationships discovered and described, and the conclusions presented, in non-statistical form.[4]

In the present study, for the sake of achieving maximum objectivity, data are presented in quantitative form whenever possible. This method of presentation is used in reporting such facts as the number of members in the organization; the number of leaders of various ranks, with their official terms of office and attendance at

[3] Queen, Stuart A., "Round Table on the Case-Study Method of Sociological Research," *Publications of the American Sociological Society*, XXII (1928), pp. 225-27.
[4] Gehlke, C. E., "The Use and Limitations of Statistics in Sociological Research," *Publications of the American Sociological Society*, XXI (1927), p. 142. See also Lindeman, E. C., *Social Discovery*, Chap. IV.

various meetings. Data as to the number of various kinds of communications (convention addresses, for example) are also presented. For such materials there is no ready-made classification, and categories have had to be inductively developed before there could be a significant enumeration. In order to supply at least sufficient objectivity so that all readers may have the same understanding of the record—and this, after all, is the final test of objective presentation—each newly made category has been defined as accurately as possible. In some instances, the technique of definition has involved not only the familiar procedure of citing synonymous terms, but also the use of case illustrations. With data that could not be satisfactorily classified, the method of complete listing has been followed.

In any case study, whether of a person or of a group or of a social movement, the rôle of investigator must, of course, be that of impartial observer, recorder, and analyst. Before undertaking such a study, the investigator must satisfy himself that he has no biases as to what the data will reveal. If he proceeds deductively, that is, if he tests "principles," or if he searches for materials to fit into a classification that has been constructed in advance, there is at least some presumption of bias, for the very act of selection of the principles to be tested or of the classifications to be used may be assumed to involve an attitude favorable to these principles and classifications. However, if the procedure is wholly inductive, as in the present study—that is, if all the available data are examined before categories are formulated, and if they are analyzed without any reference to a priori principles—the possibility of bias has been somewhat reduced.[5] Nevertheless, in the inductive as well as in the deductive attack, there must be unceasing effort to maintain the strictly objective attitude of the disinterested observer.

In any case study, the investigator must usually make some use of the historical method. Even though the emphasis is contemporaneous and factual,[6] "it is necessary to have some knowledge of the previous experiences in which the present is rooted."[7] This knowledge may be secured from the reports of competent historians, so far as such reports are available. If these do not provide an adequate

---

[5] It is, of course, not suggested that the use of established categories for the classification of data is improper under all conditions or that results secured from such a procedure are necessarily invalid. The point is merely that the selection of categories in advance carries with it a presumption as to expected outcomes and that an inductive construction of categories does not carry any such presumption.
[6] Lindeman, E. C., *op. cit.*, p. 356.
[7] Palmer, Vivien M., *op. cit.*, pp. 24-25.

Introduction

background for an understanding of the phases of group life that are rooted in "previous experience," then the investigator must turn historian and fill in the gaps, making the record [8] sufficiently complete for the purpose of his study.

The present study is not properly to be considered historical in the sense that it attempts to trace aspects of present group life back to their origins. It deals with a limited time span, this span to be thought of as a somewhat "thick" cross section in the life of the organization. Group structure, activities, and relationships, as found within this cross section, are of primary concern. Only as earlier history is essential as a background for an understanding of certain aspects of group life during this selected period has it been reported here. Even so, the method used may from one point of view quite accurately be characterized as the historical method, in that it involves "laborious research for the purposes of discovering factual material," [9] and a critical study and analysis of the material.[10]

OBJECTIVES OF THE STUDY

The objectives of the study are twofold:

1. The first objective is to furnish content for the developing field of educational sociology. This field is as yet vaguely defined, but a study of all kinds of educational organizations will undoubtedly be granted as an essential part of the special body of knowledge to be included within it. Such groups as student societies, class organizations, institutes, and teachers' associations will certainly be conceded to be a part of the raw material to which the educational sociologist may apply his techniques.

If educational sociology is to be recognized as a science, then instead of vague references and general observations concerning educational organizations, their form, their objectives, their values, it must secure data for the formulation of principles or laws which may be applied deductively. There is need, then, for a vast amount of research applied to educational organizations, as well as to other sociological aspects of the broad field of education, with the definite purpose of building up a body of special sociological data.

The attempt is made in the present study to supply not only a body of data that will be a contribution to the descriptive aspects

---

[8] *Ibid.*, pp. 23, 31.
[9] Lindeman, E. C., *op. cit.*, p. 40.
[10] Giddings, F. H., *op. cit.*, pp. 100-1.

of educational sociology as a science, but also to furnish a case illustration of the application of the method of organic sociological analysis to an educational organization. The study, then, should be of practical value to instructors and students in the developing science of educational sociology because it supplies a body of sociological information and because it illustrates the application of a method.

2. The second objective of the study is to provide an analysis of the National Education Association that will be of value to its leaders and members and perhaps to the leaders and members of educational associations in general. This aim is quite distinct from the foregoing one. It should be understood that the purpose of the study is not to reform the National Education Association. So far as the data assembled or the sociological interpretation of them may point toward a need for change, this is only an incidental outcome. It is entirely possible, however, for persons to be within an organization or a movement as leaders or members and not to be able to assume a sufficiently detached, impersonal attitude toward it to enable them to see its internal functionings and its external relationships in proper perspective. An intensive, objective, sociological analysis such as is undertaken in the present study should be a contribution in the direction of an understanding of this association on the part of such persons.

SOURCES

The sources for the study are:
1. The records of the association:
    a. Annual volumes of *Addresses and Proceedings*.
    b. *The Journal of the National Education Association*.
    c. Special bulletins and reports.
    d. News releases and form letters from headquarters of the association.
2. Secondary materials, mainly in the form of editorial and special articles in educational and general periodicals.
3. Interviews with leaders of the group.

LIMITATIONS

Certain limitations must be recognized as inherent in the very nature of the study. It is rarely, if ever, possible to make a complete report concerning a complex social group. Overt behavior may be reported, so far as it is recorded, but there may be omissions in the

Introduction 7

record. The omissions may be important or unimportant, intentional or fortuitous, continuous or occasional. Even recorded activities cannot be understood except in the light of all the factors conditioning them. Besides, some of the forces actuating a social organization in its complex activities may be inarticulate. Even after the most comprehensive and exhaustive examination, not only of the organization itself, but of the social milieu in which it is found, some significant factors may remain undiscovered.[11] This means that somewhat less than absolute validity is to be attached to the "facts" assembled in investigations of complex human groups. The implication as to the need of caution in interpreting the assembled data is clear.

The general limitations just mentioned are frankly recognized in the present study. Moreover, as already pointed out, it is impossible in this study to attempt a complete sociological analysis of such an immense group as the National Education Association because of more or less definite limitations of time and space and expense. It is necessary, therefore, to choose certain aspects of the group for treatment in this introductory study, leaving other aspects for later treatment. The aspects that should be included are those of which understanding is essential to an analysis of other aspects. Logically, since the association as a whole provides for the very existence of its subdivisions or "departments," a study of the large group should precede a study of its parts. Overt behavior of leaders and members is not capable of final interpretation until its basis in wishes, attitudes, and personal evaluations is known, but, logically, investigation and report of overt behavior must precede analysis of these personality factors which determine or condition the overt behavior. Finally, articulate elements in the social milieu should be considered before hidden or inarticulate elements, even though it may be true that the latter are just as significant as the former. The simple reason for this order of investigation is that the inarticulate elements are obviously more difficult to discover and a knowledge of the articulate factors gives needed guidance in their discovery.

The procedure, therefore, which offers the optimum values in this introductory study is believed to be the following:

1. Limit the study to the organization and activities of the association acting as a whole, omitting its subdivisions, the "departments."

[11] Cf. Counts, G. S., *School and Society in Chicago*, pp. 14-15.

2. Limit the study of wishes, attitudes, and personal evaluations on the part of leaders and members to those that are manifested in overt behavior as reported in the records.
3. In the study of the social milieu, include only those factors and conditions that are so effectively expressed as to produce overt behavior on the part of the group, omitting those which are themselves inarticulate or which fail to produce an articulate response on the part of the group.

It is believed that each of these three limitations suggests a field within which separate studies might be undertaken, and that if such studies were prosecuted they would furnish, together with the present one, a relatively comprehensive sociological analysis of the National Education Association.

CHAPTER I

THE HISTORICAL BACKGROUND OF THE NATIONAL EDUCATION ASSOCIATION

The National Teachers Association was organized August 26, 1857, at Philadelphia. It became the National Educational Association in 1870, and on February 24, 1886, it was incorporated under the laws of the District of Columbia. In 1906, the organization was incorporated under a special act of Congress as the National Education Association of the United States. The charter was accepted and by-laws were adopted at the convention held in July, 1907, in Los Angeles, California. Until 1920 the government of the association was of the town-meeting variety, all members who were in attendance at the annual conventions having a voice in the determination of policies and in the election of officers. In that year Congress amended the act of incorporation to provide (Section 12) "that said corporation may provide, by amendment to its by-laws, that the powers of the active members exercised at the annual meetings in the election of officers and the transaction of business shall be vested in, and exercised by, a representative assembly composed of delegates apportioned, elected and governed in accordance with the provisions of the by-laws adopted by said corporation." This amendment was accepted by the association at its convention in Salt Lake City, Utah, in July, 1920.[1]

Since that time, in accordance with by-laws duly adopted, the government of the organization has been a representative one.

ALEXANDER'S STUDY

Carter Alexander made a study, published in 1910, which contains an analysis of the organization and functions of the National Education Association as it existed at that time, a discussion of some of the problems facing it, and proposals for their solution.[2] It will

---

[1] *Addresses and Proceedings of the National Education Association*, 1926, pp. 1007-11.
[2] Alexander, Carter, *Some Present Aspects of the Work of Teachers' Voluntary Associations in the United States*. (Excerpts in Appendix, pp. 173-76 of the present study.)

9

be of value in orienting the reader to report some of the findings of the Alexander study.

Alexander found this association to be strictly "general" in its work. It was so general that it lacked unity—it was "a rather loose association of practically independent and highly specialized sections." At one time it became concerned lest the fact of having many sections should result in a waste of energy. It agreed to limit the number of sections to nine, but never actually imposed this limitation. It was acquiescent in the preference of some special groups of teachers to organize independently instead of as departments of the larger association.

As a result of his study Alexander urged "general associations of reasonable size with plenty of sections," these being integrated by a system of representation under which the sections would take an active part in the work of "a truly national association."

He found that the association was making little effort to influence national legislation, although upon a few issues such as the strengthening of the United States Bureau of Education, the establishment of a National University, and national aid to education, it had passed favorable resolutions and had appointed short-lived committees to present its views to the proper governmental bodies. But nothing of importance had been accomplished, due to "the usual difference of opinion and failure to take definite and continued action."

Up to 1910, according to Alexander, the association had never given much attention to efforts to advance the material welfare of teachers. It had listened to occasional addresses on the subject of teachers' salaries and had at times passed resolutions and appointed committees dealing with salaries, pensions, and tenure. In 1905 it had published a report of one of its committees dealing with these matters.

Women had not been given much recognition in the association. They held very few of the offices, and practically none of the important ones. Nor did they have any place on the general session and departmental programs. In 1910, for the first time in its history, the association elected a woman to an executive position, when it chose Mrs. Ella Flagg Young as president. Women were believed to constitute at least 75 per cent of the membership.

Alexander believed that the lack of recognition of women was not an indication of discrimination against them but was a result of their short stay in the teaching profession and of their consequent

Historical Background

lack of interest in association affairs. He saw evidences of a tendency for women to demand and to secure greater recognition.

THE PERIOD FROM 1910 TO 1917

From some points of view it would be valuable to begin the present study with the year 1910, building upon the study of Alexander. A survey of the records for the period between 1910 and 1917, however, disclosed the fact that except for the pronounced effects of the World War upon the discussions and resolutions within the association, there were no new developments of importance during these years. There were no great changes in membership, in organization, or in policy. The group continued to meet in its annual conventions, and to discuss the traditional kinds of topics. It faced from time to time the man-woman conflict within its ranks. In 1911, for example, there was a lively contest over the treasurership of the association which brought the sex representation issue out into the open. There were evidences that this issue was becoming somewhat more acute, as the following extract from an article written in 1916 will indicate:

> For years the one great association of educators of the United States has had a loosely knit membership of perhaps fifteen to twenty thousand, chiefly women classroom teachers whose half-hearted interest might be attributed to the fact that their chief privileges and duties were to furnish the audiences and to pay the dues which supported this organization.
>
> There has been an ill-concealed unrest among the rank and file of teachers, a long-standing dissatisfaction with the part assigned to them in school systems and state associations. They who are so largely responsible for the ideals and educational progress of the mass of the American people have been entirely ignored when educational policies were being formulated. . . .
>
> No longer does a grade teacher who is a member of a teachers' association carry herself with humility because of her work. She has risen fearlessly to ask for better salaries, tenure of office, an adequate pension when her services are no longer of value to her state. . . .[3]

At its conventions, the association continued to declare itself in favor of, or against, various proposals and practices, but neither the matters dealt with nor the methods of following up the resolutions seem to have changed materially. There was, however, more open attention in these declarations to the economic welfare of teachers, including salaries, tenure, and retirement allowances. In 1911 the

[3] Ortschild, Viola, "Grade Teachers Associations," *Oregon Teachers Monthly*, XXI (Sept., 1916), pp. 14-19.

resolutions called for an increase in teachers' salaries.[4] In 1915, in addition to calling for adequate salaries, there was specific reaffirmation of the need of security through tenure and a suitable retirement annuity. In addition, there was a ringing declaration in favor of peace instruction, which is reported in a supplement to the present study; a statement of the need of enlarging the scope of activity of schools, and of the need of increased funds for public education; [5] also support for increased appropriations for the United States Bureau of Education.[6] The 1916 resolutions, in addition to a statement on military training and related matters (reported in full in the supplement to the present study), included support for the following:

1. A national commission to investigate the condition of farm women and farm homes.
2. Citizenship education.
3. Federal appropriations for the education and Americanization of immigrants.
4. Woman suffrage.
5. Professional standards exclusively governing the employment of teachers and supervisors.
6. Legal definition of the powers and duties of school superintendents.
7. A minimum term of three years for superintendents.
8. Permanent tenure for teachers, properly safeguarded.
9. Salaries in keeping with professional demands.
10. Retirement allowance, state and local.[7]

These resolutions may be considered typical as to the kind and range of matters upon which the association regularly expressed itself.

Since there appears to be no significant difference between the association as Alexander described it in 1910 and the association as it existed and functioned during the years 1910 to 1917, with the exception of the differences produced by the war and its accompanying currents of thought and contagions of emotion, it seems proper to omit all intensive study of what might be considered the normal functionings of the group during these years and to record merely the adjustments made by the group to the abnormal war situation.

So far as these adjustments are related to the purposes of this study, they are reported in the succeeding chapters. In addition, in order that the historical aspects of the treatment of the National

---

[4] *Add. and Proc.*, 1911, pp. 31-33.
[5] Eventually, it was forecast, one-half of the public taxes would be required.
[6] *Add. and Proc.*, 1915, pp. 25-30.
[7] *Add. and Proc.*, 1916, pp. 27-28.

Historical Background

Education Association in the Alexander study may be brought down to the present with relative completeness, the formal expressions of the group concerning the war are reported and briefly analyzed in a supplement to the present study.[8]

THE TIME SPAN OF THE PRESENT STUDY, 1918 TO 1928

The year 1918 has been selected as the starting point of this study for several reasons. Numerous important occurrences took place about this time. The headquarters of the organization were established at the national capital, making it "possible for the Association to take a prominent part in matters of far-reaching importance."[9] A Commission on the National Emergency in Education was created. (This Commission represented the National Education Association and the Department of Superintendence, its members being appointed in 1917 and 1918.) The association began its modern agitation for a National Department of Education. The recent changes in organization, and expansions in membership and in functions and relationships are all included if the study begins with the 1918 records.

The study is carried through the records of 1928 with the desire to make it as nearly contemporaneous as possible. At the time when the data were being assembled and classified (1928 and 1929) the records for 1928 were the latest that were available.

Since the policies of the association are subject to annual determination, a period of eleven years should give ample opportunity for noting the characteristic activities of the association together with changes and continuities in structure and function.

[8] Pp. 167-72.
[9] From the 1927 report of the secretary.

CHAPTER II

EXPANSION IN MEMBERSHIP

The most outstanding development in the association during the period under discussion is the growth in membership. Up to 1917 the roster had never included as many as 10,000 names. In that year the number was 8,466; in 1918, there were 10,104 members; in 1919, more than 20,000 (accurate data not available); in 1920, 52,850; in 1921, 87,414; in 1922, 118,032; in 1923, 133,566; in 1924, 138,856; in 1925, 158,103; in 1926, 170,053; in 1927, 181,350, and in 1928, 193,145.[1]

In 1918 the membership in the association was only 1.55 per cent of the total number of teachers in public elementary and secondary schools, whereas in 1926, the latest year for which accurate data as to number of teachers are available, the percentage was 20.88. The membership in 1920 was 6.48 per cent of the total teaching population of the United States, while in 1926, 17.40 per cent of all teachers belonged.[2]

What has produced this phenomenal growth? It has resulted from certain activities carried on by the association, and from certain situations growing out of these activities: (1) There has been direct promotion of the enterprise, direct appeal to teachers to become members. (2) The membership has increased as a result of the pressure of rivalry and of tradition generated by the "100 per cent membership" plan. (3) It has increased as a result of a species of compulsion exercised upon teachers by their immediate superiors and associates. (4) There has probably been considerable increase in membership as a by-product of the reorganization of the association. (5) The greater service rendered to the individual member by the national headquarters has undoubtedly helped to retain and

---

[1] Membership figures to 1925 are from *Add. and Proc.*, 1926, p. 1163; for 1919, from *Add. and Proc.*, 1927, p. 1185, graph; for 1926, 1927, and 1928, from the Annual Report of the Secretary, *Add. and Proc.*, 1929, p. 1165. Figures for each year are recorded as of January first of following year.

[2] U. S. Bureau of Education *Bulletins:* 1922, No. 29, p. 4; 1927, No. 39, p. 3; 1928, No. 12, p. 11.

Expansion in Membership 15

to gain members. (6) The vigorous campaign for a national department of education has kept the association before the professional public and has tended to generate a favorable, loyal, appreciative attitude toward it on the part of considerable numbers of teachers.

These various activities and situations will now be considered in turn.

PROMOTION ACTIVITIES

A Commission on the National Emergency in Education was created by the executive committee of the association in 1917. This was made a joint commission of the association and the Department of Superintendence the following year, and it immediately began a plan of promotion of membership in the association by creating from among its members a Committee on the Enlistment of the Profession. This committee issued a direct appeal to the teachers of the nation in September, 1918 in the form of a pamphlet entitled *Why Educators Should Enlist in the National Education Association*. In this publication the following "professional reasons" why teachers should join the organization were enumerated: Through such an agency, it was stated, it would be possible (1) to develop among teachers a stronger consciousness of the dignity of the profession; (2) to establish a channel for the expression of the consensus of educational opinion; (3) to supply the public with correct educational information; (4) to promote an understanding of the significance of our entrance into the World War; (5) to aid in controlling the war activities of the schools; (6) to help solve the problem of adult illiteracy; (7) to show the need of more money to support public education; (8) to promote Federal aid for education; (9) to reapprehend and restate our national ideals; and (10) to restate our national program of education.

The pamphlet also listed various "personal reasons" for enlisting, namely, that it would be possible if all would join (1) to provide a means of keeping members well informed in professional matters; (2) "to make general among the members of the profession that feeling of pride and satisfaction which comes from solidarity and the knowledge that all are standing together in a spirit of mutual interest and mutual helpfulness"; (3) to promote understanding between school boards, supervisors, and teachers; (4) "to bring about, through coöperation and proper organization, such increase in the pay of teachers and such improvement in the conditions surrounding their work, as shall make it possible for them to remain in the profession and to live in a manner befitting their calling"; (5) "to permit the National Education Association to employ a permanent staff adequate to . . . assume some responsibility for influencing public opinion upon educational matters, to take an effective interest in educational legislation, national, state, and local, and to promote the interests of members, both professionally and financially."

In the *National Education Association Bulletin* for September, 1918, "Plans for the Drive" were announced. There were to be official representatives of the association in each state, namely, the State Director of the Association, the State Superintendent of Schools, the President of the State Teachers Association, and others to be appointed by these three. Superintendents of county and city schools and presidents of colleges, normal schools, and universities were designated "managers of the drive" and were asked to see to all details of securing memberships among the teachers under their direction, including the collection and transmission of membership fees.

A Field Secretary was employed from 1918 to 1924, whose principal duty was to travel throughout the country addressing groups of teachers and securing their membership in the national organization. The chairman of the Commission on the Emergency in Education also traveled widely, presenting the program of activity which the association had undertaken, and appealing to all teachers to support it. Other national, state, and local leaders in education were asked to present the issue as opportunity offered, and many volunteered to do so.

Thus at the beginning of the period under consideration there was an active campaign for members, carried on by direct appeal through printed material sent to teachers, through public addresses of paid and volunteer speakers, through personal solicitation on the part of school heads organized under state leaders. The organization was presented as one with a definite program, one with the power to deliver certain values to those who would join and to establish certain national reforms in which teachers had been conditioned through professional training to have a profound interest. Direct personal advantage was promised in the form of increased salaries, improvement in conditions surrounding the teacher's work, and information along professional lines. Less direct personal advantage was offered under such heads as achieving greater recognition of the teacher's vocation, supplying the public with correct educational information, showing the need of more money to support public education, influencing public opinion, and securing educational legislation. Somewhat remote, impersonal, or large-group values also were listed: promoting an understanding of the significance of our entrance into the World War, reapprehending and restating our national ideals, restating our national program of education, solving the problem of adult illiteracy.

The promotion of membership, the keeping of membership records, and the answering of inquiries about membership became so large a part of the work of the headquarters staff of the association that in 1925 a Division of Records and Membership was created. The first annual report of this division indicates the methods which had been found most effective in its work: [3]

> The promotion of membership falls under two more or less distinct forms: (a) promotion by mail, and (b) promotion by personal visits.
>
> ... The plans followed have been largely the same as those of past years: (a) "broadcasting" through superintendents, principals, officers of local organizations, and other recognized leaders; (b) the encouragement of schools, cities, and counties to achieve the 100 per cent goal; and (c) the life-membership campaign.
>
> ... The day is largely past, if it ever did exist, when large groups of teachers can be "inspired" into membership by the oratory of itinerant staff members. Membership in the National Education Association, as in local and state associations, is the natural result of professional vision and professional spirit. This vision and spirit are promoted primarily by professional leadership which is strongest when exerted by those who are well known and highly respected by the teachers in their respective communities, professors in schools and departments of education, superintendents, principals, and other leaders in local organizations who have caught the spirit of a real profession of teaching. Conferences between the director of this division and leaders in strategic communities, at which coöperative plans have been developed, have proved of material value and appear to be rich in possibilities for future development.

It is clear from the foregoing quotation that the prestige [4] of persons in positions of leadership continued to be utilized in creating a social opinion favorable to the association and therefore favorable to membership in it. What are the motives that impel these persons

[3] *Add. and Proc.*, 1926, pp. 1159-61.
[4] Hayes, E. C., *Introduction to the Study of Sociology*, pp. 323-24: "Every [person] has some degree of causal efficiency, as a modifier of the activities of his associates. Whatever heightens the causal efficiency of an individual or of a class so as to make that individual or class more effective as the source of social suggestion, radiation and imitation is said to give prestige." Cf. Bogardus, E. S., *Fundamentals of Social Psychology*, p. 136.

to lend their efforts and their prestige in the promotion of this enterprise? The wish for public recognition lends itself to exploitation in such a situation as this, in that there is a promise of becoming known as a group leader.[5] The wish for security also may be appealed to indirectly in that each leader who coöperates is made to feel that his occupational group has its status to safeguard. In the circular letters which are sent to superintendents and principals seeking their coöperation in securing members, there is a consistent use of direct and indirect suggestion involving both public recognition and security. For example, a letter sent to city and county superintendents under date of August 10, 1928, reads, in part, as follows:

> We are inclosing material which we will send to principals on September 10. We are sure of your fullest support in this unparalleled development of the profession. Superintendents have not failed us and we trust we have not failed them. The biggest thing any superintendent can do is to inspire principals and teachers with a desire to be an active force in the profession. You are doing that. Because of your interest and work we feel free to call on you for help.
>
> Here is what we want you to do at this time:
>
> 1. Send or have your secretary send us a list of the changes in the principalships in your schools or else send a complete list. Do this if possible before September 1.
> 2. Encourage your principals to try for the honor roll of 100 per cent schools, as soon as the schools open.
> 3. Call on us for additional enlistment supplies as you need them. Call on us for points of information on this question and on that one.
>
> Have you not observed the increase of professional interest on the part of principals and teachers? No other profession has the teamwork and the success that we now have. If we can keep this going and growing, the wonderful achievements of the last decade will be more than doubled in the next decade. It pays for every superintendent in both city and county to have his shoulder to the wheel. This is the time for a reaction as to salaries and tenure which only continuous teamwork can avert. The reaction actually started a year ago but it seems to be crumbling as it goes up against solidarity and harmony in the profession.
>
> At your teachers' meetings call attention to the progress which is being made as a result of teamwork in the activities of the profession. Show what it means to teachers locally and nationally. Show what it means to the schools of the land. It is necessary to do this, for, being in the current as we are in this, the greatest educational movement of the age, we may not fully appreciate, if left alone, the rate of progress that is being made and we may not realize the help that each can give.

[5] In his study, *The Unadjusted Girl* (pp. 1-40), W. I. Thomas formulates and illustrates the concept of the "wishes": the wish for security, the wish for new experience, the wish for personal response, the wish for public recognition.

Expansion in Membership

Let teachers and principals be conscious of what is taking place and conscious of the help they are giving. That develops professional pride, and increasing professional pride stabilizes the work on higher and higher levels.

This letter was followed on September 10 by one addressed to principals, which read, in part, as follows:

> Many thousands have expressed appreciation for the series of letters to principals last year. They claim that these letters were inspirational and that they contained valuable information. These reports encourage us to try to be of still greater help this year. Being in touch with the teachers and principals of the nation, as we are, we ought to be able to render a clearing-house service of value to all.
>
> This first letter must of course contain suggestions for the most effective membership drive in the history of the association. In the next letter we plan to mention observations on The Principal the Key to Professional Progress. If principals could see and know what we know from contacts throughout the nation they would be mighty proud of their leadership and what it is actually accomplishing.

It is, of course, evident that the aim in these letters is to secure the active coöperation of school officials in a membership campaign. What the superintendents are asked to do is indicated very directly: to send names, to encourage principals to act, to send for supplies and information, to call teachers' attention to progress. The verbal setting in which this request for coöperation is placed furnishes indirect suggestion of recognition of the recipients of the letters. The fact that these communications place in their hands a certain responsibility for continuing "the unparalleled development of the profession" and being leaders in the "greatest educational movement of the age" carries the implication that they are important persons. They are indirectly recognized as being somewhat responsible for the past and present success of the "movement" since the implication is that they have taken part in the teamwork which has brought success. In the letter sent to principals September 10, there is the most obvious use of indirect suggestion to appeal to their wish for public recognition: "If principals could see and know what we know from contacts throughout the nation they would be mighty proud of their leadership and what it is actually accomplishing."

The wish for security is exploited by the indirect suggestion, throughout the first letter, that there have been accomplishments of great value through association activity. "Success"; "wonderful achievements"; "reaction as to salaries and tenure . . . . crumbling"; "solidarity and harmony"; "progress"—these expressions suggest professional security to be gained and maintained through aiding in the "movement." "Show what it means" implies that it means much. "It pays for every superintendent ... to have his shoulder to the wheel" suggests both security and public recognition to be gained.

Since the suggestions are largely indirect, they are more likely to be effective in securing the desired behavior than if they were direct, for according to Sidis, "A suggestion is more effective the more indirect it is, and in proportion as it becomes direct it loses its efficacy." [6] At least indirect suggestion is more effective than direct suggestion, if the suggested behavior lies close to, or within, the field of habitual behaviors and attitudes, as it manifestly does in the present instance.[7]

It is idle to discuss the question of whether the statements in these letters concerning the association represent actual conditions or whether they are a reflection of "wishful thinking." In the absence of the application of objective methods of evaluation, it is impossible to know whether this is the "greatest educational movement of the age" or not. For present purposes it is sufficient to note that this assertion and others similar to it are included in communications that are sent out for the purpose of securing the coöperation of school officials in membership drives, and that they are in the nature of indirect suggestion for behavior to satisfy the wishes for security and for public recognition.

Although the suggestions for action are indirect in the main, they are worded "in a positive rather than a negative manner." There is no hint of doubt or failure. This fact adds to their effectiveness.[8]

RIVALRY AND TRADITION AS FACTORS IN EXPANSION

The 100 per cent membership slogan has been very much stressed by the association. *The Journal of the National Education Association,* a periodical which is received by all members of the organization, prints the list of 100 per cent schools each month—that is, the names of the school buildings within which all the teachers are members of the association. It also prints the list of cities and counties in which all the teachers are members. Here is a clear case of an appeal to group loyalty and the securing of a result through rivalry among groups. If the teachers in School A, in the city of X,

---

[6] Sidis, B., *The Psychology of Suggestion,* p. 52.
[7] Bogardus. E. S., *op. cit.,* pp. 125-32.
[8] Allport, F. H., *Social Psychology,* p. 251.

Expansion in Membership

are publicly recognized for their professional devotion in that all of them have joined the national professional organization, the teachers of School B in the same city, if there is any sense of loyalty to School B and especially if other relationships with School A have aroused a spirit of rivalry, will in all probability gladly spend the two dollars per person necessary to secure membership, and thus avoid being outdone by another group of teachers. Although there would perhaps not be so keen a rivalry between cities and counties as between school staffs within the same city, there would be at least the element of rivalry and it would have its effect upon the growth of the membership list.

Arousing a spirit of rivalry among groups is a commonly practiced means for securing a desired outcome and many sociologists and social psychologists have noted its efficacy. According to Cooley, "Human rivalry appears to have [an] . . . instinctive element in it; to become aware of life and striving going on about us seems to act immediately on the nerves, quickening an impulse to live and strive in like manner. . . . The motive of rivalry, then, is a strong sense that there is a race going on, and an impulsive eagerness to be in it. . . . Rivalry supplies a stimulus wholesome and needful to the great majority of men and . . . is, on the whole, a chief progressive force, utilizing the tremendous power of ambition and controlling it to the furtherance of ends that are socially approved. . . ."[9]

Ross notes the practice of "pitting gang against gang, shop against shop, branch office against branch office, school against school, battleship against battleship . . ." and finds the device effective.[10]

Vincent has called rivalry "essentially a struggle for status, for social prestige, for the approval of inclusive publics which form the spectators for such contests."[11] Allport believes that when groups rather than individuals are involved in competition there is ". . . an exhilarating excitement in the feeling of magnified conquest. It is pleasant to win a personal contest; but it is little short of sublime to be a member of a victorious group."[12] An attitude of cooperation is combined with one of rivalry.

That the stimulation of rivalry has been effective in the National

---

[9] Cooley, C. H., *Human Nature and the Social Order*, pp. 305-7.
[10] Ross, E. A., *Principles of Sociology*, pp. 266-67.
[11] Vincent, G. E., "The Rivalry of Social Groups," *American Journal of Sociology*, XVI (1910-1911), pp. 471-84.
[12] Allport, F. H., *op. cit.*, p. 282.

Education Association campaigns for members may be seen from the increase in the number of 100 per cent schools. From approximately 1,300 in 1921-1922, the year when the plan was put into effect, the number had risen to a total of more than 5,000 in 1926-1927.

Eventually, when a particular school has had an unbroken record of 100 per cent membership for a number of years, the staff for a particular year will be influenced to continue the unbroken record not only by the desire to equal or surpass other schools but by the force of tradition as well. Tradition may be defined as an "aspect of the psycho-social environment [which] . . . preserves the psychic technique and attitudes of the past." [13] According to Ellwood, "it is the tradition of the group . . . which accounts very largely for the behavior of the individual member of the group, especially when he is consciously acting as a member of the group." [14] Tradition, as conceived by Keller, is the factor in societal evolution corresponding to heredity in organic evolution. "Heredity in nature," he says, "causes the offspring to resemble or repeat the present type; tradition in societal evolution causes the mores of one period to repeat those of the preceding period." [15] The pattern of the behavior of all newcomers is likely to be found in the traditions of the group which they enter.[16]

The program of stimulation of rivalry, as practiced by the National Education Association, includes not only the reporting of 100 per cent schools year by year in the columns of the monthly *Journal* but the special mention of those having a record for two or more years consecutively. It is clear that the rivalry technique will eventually be reënforced in some schools, if indeed this is not even now the case, by what may properly be called a tradition of 100 per cent membership.

MEMBERSHIP UNDER COMPULSION

There is a tendency for any group to practice a degree of nonviolent coercion to cause its individual members to conform to its standards and to coöperate in its collective enterprises. Ogburn observes that "Collective effort towards the doing of anything, other than the simplest like response to stimuli, involves teamwork and

---

[13] Bernard, L. L., "The Psychological Foundations of Society," in *An Introduction to Sociology*, by Davis, Barnes, and Others, p. 416.
[14] Ellwood, C. A., *The Psychology of Human Society*, p. 197.
[15] Keller, A. G., *Societal Evolution*, pp. 212-15.
[16] Ellwood, C. A., *loc. cit.*

coöperation. The individual who interferes with such collective effort will tend to experience in some form of expression the resentment of the group."[17] Giddings refers to the development of social pressure as illustrated in money-raising drives, and declares that "the modes that it has assumed . . . are numerous and many of them are highly coercive."[18] The 100 per cent membership drive tends to develop the same kinds of coercion that are developed in a money-raising drive, the effective element in each situation being the feeling of the individual that the group is resentful of his lack of coöperation. His wish for security, for the feeling that he is fully accepted and approved by the group, leads him to coöperate.[19] In a teaching staff in which a spirit of rivalry has been aroused, and especially if 100 per cent membership in the association has become traditional, a newcomer would no doubt find it very difficult to go contrary to group expectation in the matter of acquiring membership, for in this situation the pressures would be relatively strong and persistent.

There is still another aspect of the membership campaigns that imposes a degree of compulsion upon some teachers. Alexander reported in 1910 that "many women join state associations and even the National Education Association practically under compulsion from their superintendents."[20] The association now works through superintendents and principals in the securing of memberships and in many instances the teachers' membership fees are transmitted by these officials. The officials themselves are more or less actuated by the spirit of rivalry that is produced by publishing the names of 100 per cent schools. In this situation, even though, so far as is known, there is no formal requirement anywhere that teachers join the association, they will feel under considerable constraint to join it if a superior officer lets it be known that he desires a 100 per cent record for his school, and if he is in a position to know who does and who does not coöperate in the attainment of this goal.

REORGANIZATION OF THE ASSOCIATION

When the association reorganized in 1920, it adopted a scheme for the "affiliation" of local and state associations with the national body. This not only brought it to the attention of the members of

[17] Ogburn, W. F., *Social Change*, p. 182.
[18] Giddings, F. H., *Studies in the Theory of Human Society*, p. 266.
[19] Thomas, W. I., *op. cit.*, pp. 1-40.
[20] Alexander, Carter, *op. cit.*, p. 208.

these smaller organizations, through the discussion of the proposed relationship and of the advantages of a coördination of the work of all the regional and specialized professional groups, but, once the very simple arrangement had been entered into, these groups were expected to elect delegates to the newly created Representative Assembly of the National Association. This brought the members of these groups into a much closer relationship with the association through the reports given by delegates upon their return. Whereas the national body had been wholly secondary in character for the great mass of teachers, it now became intermediate through this direct representation for all who were at once members of an affiliated group and members of the larger group.[21] In a face-to-face report the enthusiasm of the large convention could be transmitted to teachers everywhere by returned delegates much more effectively than it could be by a bulletin or by a volume of *Addresses and Proceedings*. Those who had been most alert and active in the smaller organizations tended thus to become and to remain members of the larger organization and to become effective promoters of its appeal for members.

SERVICE TO THE MEMBERSHIP

(There are certain objective returns to the individual member in exchange for the fee that he pays. First, there is *The Journal*, a periodical of sixty-four pages at present, which is sent to all members nine times a year. The variety and the extent of the services which the association attempts to render to the members through this medium are reported in some detail in a later chapter.[22] Second, the headquarters staff supplies information along educational lines to individual members of the association upon request. Third, the association gathers and publishes, sometimes in separate bulletins, data of interest to the individual members in such practical matters as salary, tenure, and retirement allowances. Fourth, the payment of the membership fee secures the privilege of attendance at all conventions of the association, and it secures a reduced railroad rate for the journey to the place of meeting.

It is undoubtedly true that some teachers pay the membership fee of two dollars at a particular time because at that time the practical value of one or more of the foregoing services is felt to be more

---

[21] Smith, W. R., *Principles of Educational Sociology*, pp. 91-92.
[22] Chap. VI.

Expansion in Membership

than two dollars. The act of joining the association in such cases is purely a business transaction—a purchase of services or materials or privileges.

In addition to these objective returns in exchange for the membership fee, there are other values, more or less intangible and subjective, which may be related to the fact of growth of the membership list. Evidence that those engaged in membership promotion believe that these intangible values exist is to be found in the inclusion of the item, "consciousness of membership," in the list of "Privileges to Members" printed on the reverse side of the card which is issued to each person who becomes a member. Additional evidence of the belief that such values may have an effect upon the success of membership campaigns is to be found in the pamphlet issued by the Committee on the Enlistment of the Profession.[23] Among the "personal reasons" for joining the association, this committee included: "To make general among the members of the profession the feeling of pride and satisfaction which comes from solidarity and the knowledge that all are standing together in a spirit of mutual interest and mutual helpfulness."

THE CAMPAIGN FOR A NATIONAL DEPARTMENT OF EDUCATION

A Commission on the National Emergency in Education was created in 1917 and 1918, as already noted. This commission issued pronouncements which, in substance and in tone, were calculated to make the teachers of the nation aware of the existence of a multiple crisis in American education. "Our schools are in danger," asserted one of the earliest resolutions.[24] This arresting declaration was supported by such expressions as ". . . instruct five million illiterates" ". . . Americanize thirteen million foreigners" ". . . pay teachers a living wage" ". . . Present situation is critical . . ." "Immediate national aid is urgently needed . . ." Other statements of leaders were similarly startling in tone. In an address at the 1918 convention of the association the chairman of the Emergency Commission declared the "situation truly alarming" and urged that "we need to undertake a crusade." He referred to the "miserable salaries" of teachers. He cited the fact that great numbers of teachers were untrained, that normal schools were poorly supported, and that our

---
[23] See p. 15 of the present study.
[24] Joint resolution of Committee on Salaries, Pensions, and Tenure and the Commission on the National Emergency in Education, adopted by the association at its 1918 convention. *Add. and Proc.*, 1918, pp. 762-63.

great immigrant population was in need of education.[25] This same leader, as president of the association, reported at the convention a year later that progress was being made, yet he declared, "We are face to face with a great crisis." Concluding his address, he said, "We are enlisted in a great cause. We seek to perpetuate the democratic institutions in the defense of which we pledged our lives, our fortunes, and our sacred honor. . . ."[26] These statements, and others similar in tone, all of them containing facts and figures in support of the leaders' declarations of crisis, were distributed throughout the nation.

"Our schools are in danger" or "The nation is in danger" may be said to represent the alleged crisis in general terms as it was defined by these leaders. In detail, as they defined it, the crisis included illiteracy, the lack of a program of Americanization of the foreign-born, poorly paid teachers, inadequately trained teachers, meagerly supported normal schools, extreme inequality of educational opportunity. Whether teachers, before these pronouncements were made, were conscious of all these conditions, and whether they considered that they constituted a crisis, are questions that cannot be answered with assurance. There was at least a quite general and deeply rooted unrest due to the fact that teachers' salaries had not been adjusted to keep pace with war-time living costs. There is abundant evidence that the salary situation was critical and that dissatisfaction was widespread. Both educational and general periodicals printed much material dealing with the problem, and this would have the effect of intensifying the feeling of dissatisfaction. The following is typical of the kind of material commonly printed and dealing with the economic disadvantages under which teachers were laboring:

> High school boys employed in the summer of 1919 as machinists' helpers in the shipyards of a Virginia city received more per day than did the elementary teachers of the city. . . . Elementary teachers in New York City—where teachers' salaries are relatively high—receive practically the same wage as butchers, chauffeurs, clerks, waiters, etc., almost none of whom require special preparation for their work. . . . According to the union scale of wages operative in 1918 in a geographical district in which Cleveland and Chicago were selected as representative industrial cities, head bakers received $363 more per year than the elementary teachers of the same district, blacksmiths $860 more and machinists $1,138 more. . . . The increase in

---

[25] Strayer, George D., "The Present Emergency in Education," *Add. and Proc.*, 1918, pp. 205-7.

[26] Strayer, George D., "The National Education Association Program of Work," *Add. and Proc.*, 1919, pp. 41-46.

Expansion in Membership

teachers' salaries between 1914-1915 and 1918 is . . . entirely inadequate to meet the advance in the cost of living. . . .[27]

As to the other conditions to which the commission directed attention, awareness of them and attitudes toward them would no doubt vary widely, depending upon variety of training and upon extent of direct and indirect contacts with the situations that were cited. In any case, whether teachers were aware of the existence of a crisis before the commission's pronouncements or whether these statements constituted the first evidence of the existence of a crisis, there developed what, from the sociological point of view, was a typical crowd situation,[28] and this fact had its effect upon the growth of the association. There was a *crisis situation*. There was unrest and more or less *"milling"* (through discussion) in search of a solution. *Leaders* came forward to *define the situation* and to *concentrate attention upon one objective* as a solution of the several aspects of the crisis. The solution proposed was the creation of a federal department of education subsidized sufficiently by Congress so that it could deal effectively with the problems.[29] To achieve this objective, the leaders declared that it was important that all teachers join the National Education Association. It is impossible to determine the number of persons who have joined the association because of the feeling and the heightened suggestibility characteristic of crowds, as compared with the number who have joined because of a rational conclusion concerning the professional values to be cooperatively achieved through membership. But there is some evidence that the crowd spirit in the association has been relatively strong and continuous in relation to the proposal to establish a National Department of Education. The almost unanimous reaffirmation at the annual conventions of the demand for the establishment of such a department is in itself evidence in this direction. *Intolerance of difference of response*, a crowd characteristic, has been ob-

---

[27] "Teachers' Salaries and the Wages for Unskilled Labor," *School and Society*, XI, pp. 176-77 (Feb. 7, 1920), quoting from the *Monthly Labor Review*.
[28] Kulp, D. H., II, *Outlines of the Sociology of Human Behavior*, Chap. XXXIII. Park, R. E. and Burgess, E. W., *Introduction to the Science of Sociology*, Chap. XIII.
[29] It was not proposed that the federal government should participate directly in increasing teachers' salaries. The Committee on the Enlistment of the Profession did, however, point out the prospect of bringing about, "through coöperation and proper organization, such increase in the pay of teachers and such improvement in the conditions surrounding their work, as shall make it possible for them to remain in the profession and to live in a manner befitting their calling." The interests of members were to be promoted "both professionally and financially." (Pp. 15-16 of present study.)

servable. These facts are cited later in the present study.[30] They are noted here merely because of their bearing upon the probability that crowd sociology has affected the size of the association. The assumption is that in connection with this one issue at least—the creation of a National Department of Education—crowd attitudes and behaviors have had something to do with teachers becoming and remaining members of the association.

SOCIAL CONDITIONINGS IN THE SITUATION

All the foregoing activities and situations have doubtless been somewhat effective in the production of a particular kind of behavior, namely, formal membership of teachers in this organization. If all elements in the teachers' situation had remained as they were in 1917 and earlier, except for the influences just cited, a favorable response from many teachers would have been the logical result. That is, many would certainly have joined the group. But at the beginning of the period of this study, there were certain unusual social conditionings which must have operated to increase the effectiveness of these efforts and influences:

Familiarity with Promotion Schemes. During the World War teachers became accustomed to propagandists' appeals designed to secure their participation in many movements. The Red Cross, the Junior Red Cross, thrift, food conservation, purchase of government bonds—these and numerous other movements and activities were presented in rapid succession. Teachers and others were more or less in the habit of paying serious attention to public appeals.

Familiarity with Compulsion. Social pressure was exerted on all persons, teachers along with the rest, to cause them to participate in movements such as those just mentioned, dealing with various national problems. Subscriptions, memberships, and contributions were reported through employers and through superiors in rank. Names were published, quotas were assigned, 100 per cent participation was cited. Compulsion was widely practiced and approved.

Emotionalized Attitudes Toward National Needs. There was an increase of loyalty and devotion to the nation. This being the case, the mere presentation of illiteracy, inequality of educational opportunity, etc., as aspects of a great national crisis, would tend to result in whatever behavior was suggested by the leaders as appropriate in the crisis. In this case the leaders urged the joining of an organiza-

[30] Pp. 135-37.

tion that was committed to the meeting of the crisis through agitation for national governmental activity and subsidy. Moreover, the leaders exploited wartime stereotypes as techniques of suggestion, as, for example, in the use of such terms as emergency, crisis, danger.

The Economic Crisis for Teachers. Teachers' incomes were seriously inadequate.[31] They tended to seek a solution of this critical situation in many ways, among the methods being the formation of new organizations and the support of organizations already in existence, if they promised to attack the problem, as the National Education Association did.

The Desire for Social Status of the Teacher's Vocation. Associated with the economic issue was the less acutely felt issue of social recognition of the occupation of teaching. It is impossible to determine the strength or prevalence of this wish for improved status. But so far as it was a live issue, it conditioned teachers to respond favorably to the association's campaign for members, for the association was undertaking to secure official recognition of education in the national government.

This whole situation furnishes an excellent illustration of the effect of conjunctivity in an array of social conditions. Because of their occurrence in close time proximity, these various conditions produced the striking social phenomenon of rapid and extreme growth in an organization which had been maintaining itself on a relatively low and quite uniform level of numerical strength for more than half a century. This result came about because this organization defined the teacher's crisis and suggested that teachers meet it by joining the National Education Association.

The special war-time conditionings may be assumed to have ceased to be effective or at least to have been weakened toward the end of the period of this study. But they were effective for a long enough time to accomplish a great increase in numerical strength, and this factor of great size is itself likely to influence the behavior of many persons. The tendency is for individual judgments and choices to conform to what large numbers of persons are known to have done.[32] Moreover, compulsion has been continued by virtue of the continuance of the method of approach to prospective members through their superiors in school systems. Rivalry is effective in peace time as well as in war time, and it is still used as a promotion device.

[31] See p. 26 of the present study.
[32] Allport, F. H., *op. cit.*, pp. 249-50. Cf. Sidis, B., *op. cit.*, Part III

Traditions of 100 per cent membership from particular schools become more effective as the number of years of perfect record increases. Teachers are probably just as much concerned about social recognition of their vocation in peace time as in war time; hence are as favorably conditioned to the support of a campaign for official governmental recognition as they ever were. They respond as readily as ever to proposals to furnish objective values in the form of service and information, and these values continue to be furnished by the association.

It is probable that the promotion schemes are not equally effective in all classes of teachers. Officials in charge of promotion believe [33] that elementary teachers in villages and cities are more largely represented in the membership than high school teachers, and certainly that rural teachers are relatively much less numerous than either of these other groups. They believe that normal school teachers are comparatively well represented, but teachers in other professional schools and in colleges of liberal arts have not joined in large numbers. It should be evident that teachers in rural schools cannot be reached successfully by any of the indirect methods of promotion thus far used except in the parts of the country where there is a county or township organization of rural schools, for it is only in organized groups that compulsion and rivalry can be effectively utilized. It is doubtful whether college and university teachers can be reached by the methods of direct promotion, rivalry, and compulsion. In fact, an attempt to apply these methods among college and university groups might produce wholly negative results not only in the form of failure to secure members, but also in the form of the arousal of open resistance and active opposition. Even in the absence of data as the basis for a conclusion in the matter, it will probably be agreed that there is a tradition of independence in college teaching not found in other branches of the teaching service. Certainly there is greater average maturity. The degree of specialization is greater. The proportion of men on this level is greater than on other levels. These conditions make it at least doubtful whether the methods found successful in securing members in elementary and secondary ranks can be made to work satisfactorily in this higher rank. It is conceivable that the social distance between college and university teachers on the one hand and rural and elementary teachers on the other hand might make it somewhat inadvisable to include

[33] Personal communication.

these classes in miscellaneous fashion in the same organization, even if it were possible to do so. Feelings of superiority and inferiority are involved, as well as diverse specialized professional interests, different kinds and degrees of training, and differences in prestige.[34] It is beyond the scope of this study to attempt to determine the degree of social distance between classes of teachers, or to discover its importance in conditioning the response of certain classes to promotion schemes. It is merely pointed out incidentally here that this is a promising field for investigation, not only because of its general sociological interest, but also because of its practical significance for those who carry on membership promotion activities.

The promotion activities of the National Education Association are manifestly on a basis of extreme inclusiveness. There is no selection of members; there is no preliminary examination or preparation of prospective members; there is no probationary period, no initiation. All who pay the annual fee of two dollars are welcomed as members. A question may well be raised as to the strength of a social organization that is so broadly inclusive in its membership, and especially when such devices as rivalry and compulsion are used to increase and maintain the membership list. The association, under these conditions, has within it not only those who have joined because of appreciation of the values to be found in its program of work, but also some who are indifferent to it and no doubt some who are resentful of a situation which has compelled them to become members against their will. These last two classes can be considered a source of strength to the organization only because they increase its financial income and because they help to create an impression of size, with the implication that size carries with it as to social acceptability. But their membership provides no assurance of unity or of stability in the organization or of coöperation in any of the enterprises in which the association is engaged. If the act of joining were wholly spontaneous, in no case involving any element of artificially created influence, the association might have difficulty in maintaining its numerical strength, but it would be assured of a degree of solidarity which is highly problematical under present conditions of promotional activity.

[34] Park, R. E., and Burgess, E. W., *op. cit.*, Chap. IV.
Counts, G. S., "The Social Status of Occupations," *School Review*, XXXIII (Jan., 1925), pp. 16-27.
Bogardus, E. S., "Social Distance and its Origins," *Journal of Applied Sociology*, IX (Jan., 1925), pp. 216-26.

Without going into the question of the need for a general national association of teachers such as the National Education Association or of the need for any kind of association for that matter, it may be pointed out in passing that, if it is highly desirable from the individual or from the professional or from the broad social point of view that teachers should join one or more professional organizations, it should be possible to achieve this result as one of the outcomes of what would be called, sociologically, the process of occupational acculturation. Most of those who enter the occupation of teaching do so by way of a special training for their work. During the course of this training they are gradually inducted into the occupational culture—the special skills, tools, ideas, and attitudes—of the teaching "craft." If professional organization has values, it would obviously be proper for teacher-training schools to develop in prospective teachers such an appreciation of these values that they would seek membership in a professional organization. No data are available to prove that teacher-training faculties believe these values to exist; but if they do exist, such an association as the National Education Association should be able to demonstrate the fact and to induce these institutions to stress their importance during the period of acculturation. The present would seem to be a propitious time for attempting to secure the coöperation of these professional schools in this matter, for the period is one of transition from a two-year to a four-year program of work in many of them.

The conditioning of teachers in training, as here proposed, so that they would appreciate the values, immediate and remote, tangible and intangible, which are to be realized through participation in professional organization, should have the practical effect of decreasing the amount of artificial promotion required to produce the present result in membership, or of producing a larger result from the same amount of promotional activity. Moreover, regardless of the quantitative result, it may be predicted with some confidence that if membership were to spring from an advance interest in the association, this interest having come in turn as a natural outcome of the process of training, the association would have more assurance of stability and solidarity as well as keener interest and more active participation in its affairs on the part of the members. In other words, membership which is the natural result of a process of conditioning would be more satisfactory than membership resulting from the imposition of artificial controls.

Expansion in Membership

THE LIFE MEMBERSHIP PLAN

In addition to the continual campaign for the "enlistment" of teachers in the association and for their renewal of memberships annually through the payment of the fee of two dollars, an active effort has been made since 1921 to secure life members. It is unlikely that this effort results in adding to the total membership, for those who have sufficient interest in the organization to enroll as life members would be certain to pay the annual fee if they did not pay the life fee of $100. However, these life membership fees are added to the permanent fund and are not used for current expenses, thus increasing the stability of the organization if not affecting its size. The only possibility of adding to the number of members comes from the fact that an occasional teacher who would not himself enroll may have a life membership presented as a gift from his associates.[35] The decision in 1926 to permit the payment of the life membership fee in ten annual installments has resulted in a marked increase in the number of persons desiring such membership. Eight hundred names were added to the list in 1927-1928, bringing the total to approximately 1,800.

The methods used in inducing teachers to become life members are quite similar to those used in attracting new members. There is exploitation of the desire for status within the organization and of the desire to advance the status of the teaching profession. There is a direct appeal through local leaders who are asked to invite teachers to take out this permanent membership. Personal rivalry is stimulated by the publication of the names of life members in *The Journal* and until 1925 in the annual volume of *Addresses and Proceedings*. Groups are set against one another—in this case, state against state; for example, in 1928, Pennsylvania, Ohio, California, and Texas were encouraged to compete against one another in the securing of these memberships. In addition to these methods, which, as stated, are quite similar to the schemes used in the campaign for annual memberships, other devices are in use. An attempt has been made to form a "membership chain," each new life member securing one other.[36] A specially designed gold pin may be worn by the life member, and there is a strong probability that in the near future there will be a key, similar in design to those worn by the members

---

[35] Secretary's Report, *Add. and Proc.*, 1928, p. 1146.
[36] *Loc. cit.*

of honorary scholastic fraternities.[37] This is a very obvious appeal to the wish for public recognition. In the same direction is the suggestion of exclusiveness. Those who are soliciting life members are directed to "pick out only those who will do credit to this distinguished list." [38]

A suggestion as to the strength of the wish for public recognition is to be found in the statement of the secretary of the association: "Many who accept the life membership invitation have great difficulty in making ends meet. They make a financial sacrifice in accepting and in paying their notes each year. The joy, satisfaction, and prestige that come, according to their reports, more than compensate them for the outlay and for the sacrifices made." [39] There may be a considerable element of rationalization or "wishful thinking" in such a declaration as this, both in the reports coming from life members and in this official interpretation of the reports. But whether a rationalization or a carefully considered statement of fact, the declaration has significance as a stereotype exploited for suggestion in the membership propaganda.

[37] Since this was written, the key has been authorized.
[38] In a circular letter from the Washington headquarters, Sept. 1, 1928.
[39] Secretary's Report, *Add. and Proc.*, 1928, p. 1146.

CHAPTER III

ORGANIZATION OF THE NATIONAL EDUCATION ASSOCIATION

Until 1920 the National Education Association was an organization of the town-meeting type. At its annual business meeting, all active members, that is, all persons who were engaged in educational work and who had paid their membership dues for the current year, were entitled to vote on all issues, and all were eligible to hold office.[1] At this meeting, the president, eleven vice-presidents,[2] the treasurer, and one director from each state, territory, and district were elected by ballot by a majority vote of the active members present, the term of all these officers being one year.

The Act of Incorporation prescribed the form of organization under which these elected officers, as well as an additional one, the secretary, should function.[3] There was, first, a Board of Directors, made up of elected members from the various states, territories, and districts as mentioned in the preceding paragraph, and including also: the president of the association; the first vice-president of the association, that is, the retiring president; the secretary of the association; the treasurer; the chairman of the Board of Trustees; and life directors in the persons of the Commissioner of Education of the United States, and all past presidents of the association.[4] The Board of Directors should have in charge, it was prescribed, "the general interests of the corporation, excepting those herein intrusted to the Board of Trustees."

There was, secondly, an Executive Committee composed of five members: the president, the first vice-president, the treasurer, the chairman of the Board of Trustees, and one member of the association chosen annually by the Board of Directors. This committee was to act for the Board of Directors in the intervals between

---
[1] By-laws, Article I, Section 6.
[2] The retiring president became first vice-president. The number of vice-presidents thus is twelve.
[3] Section 6.
[4] In addition to these, certain persons and institutions that had paid a life membership fee in the 1880's were made life directors and continue to be so listed.

the meetings of that body. The secretary of the association was secretary of this committee.

Thirdly, there was a Board of Trustees. This consisted of four members elected by the Board of Directors for a term of four years, and a fifth member, the president of the association, ex officio. This board was charged with the safekeeping and investment of the Permanent Fund, and of all other funds which the corporation might receive as gifts. It also elected the secretary of the association for a term not to exceed four years.

The provision which made the active members who happened to attend the annual business meeting the governing body of the organization was very unsatisfactory. Such a body could not be held responsible to the teaching profession as a whole. Those voting were nameless holders of membership cards. The meetings were criticized as being too large for the expeditious transaction of business and on the other hand they were criticized for not being large enough to be representative of the teachers of the country as a whole, and of being "run" by a small minority. Whereas the charter was supposed to provide a strictly democratic method of governing the association, in practice the method turned out to be highly undemocratic in many instances, for a local or regional group frequently outnumbered those from all other parts of the country and, if organized for the purpose, such a group could elect whatever officers it chose and could put the organization behind its own special program.

Finally, after considerable preliminary discussion at conventions and in the educational press, a specific proposal for changing from the town-meeting type to a delegate type of governing body was made at the annual convention in 1918, but not brought to a vote at that time; it was submitted again in 1919, but blocked by an organized group of teachers; it was again submitted at the 1920 convention, held far away from the centers of population at Salt Lake City, Utah, and was there adopted after a sharp fight.[5]

The present organization is represented graphically in the chart on page 37.

THE REPRESENTATIVE ASSEMBLY

The reorganization did not affect the Board of Directors or the Executive Committee or the Board of Trustees in any way, and

[5] "The Reorganized National Education Association," *School Review*, XXVIII (Sept., 1920), pp. 481-86.

Organization of Association

A GRAPHIC REPRESENTATION OF THE ORGANIZATION OF THE NATIONAL EDUCATION ASSOCIATION

N.E.A. MEMBERS — WHO ARE MEMBERS OF AFFILIATED ORGANIZATIONS

REPRESENTATIVE ASSEMBLY — ACTUAL MEMBERSHIP — 800-1150; POTENTIAL MEMBERSHIP — 2000

BOARD OF DIRECTORS — STATE AND TERRITORIAL DIRECTORS — 54; ASSOCIATION OFFICERS — 5; LIFE DIRECTORS — VARYING

NATIONAL COUNCIL OF EDUCATION * — 120; PLUS THREE FROM EACH DEPARTMENT

EXECUTIVE COMMITTEE — 5

BOARD OF TRUSTEES — 5

SECRETARY

HEADQUARTERS STAFF — 100 TO 150 PERSONS; 8 DIVISIONS

Divisions: ACCOUNTS, LEGISLATIVE, RESEARCH, BUSINESS, PUBLICATIONS, CLASSROOM SERVICE, ADMINISTRATIVE SERVICE (DEPT. OF SUPERINTENDENCE), RECORDS AND MEMBERSHIP

18 DEPARTMENTS

SPECIAL COMMITTEES

KEY
——— CREATIVE AND APPOINTIVE
– – – COOPERATIVE AND ADVISORY
⋯⋯ INTERLOCKING
* THE NATIONAL COUNCIL IS PARTIALLY SELF-PERPETUATING

their place in the structure is adequately described in the brief references in the preceding paragraphs. The fundamental change was the creation of a Representative Assembly. The structure and relationships of this body will require somewhat amplified description. This will also be true of the departments, the executive staff, the committees and commissions, as well as the National Council of Education.

The place of the Representative Assembly in the reorganized association is indicated in the following sections of the amended by-laws:

Article II

Section 1. The election of officers and transaction of business at the annual business meeting shall be by a Representative Assembly composed of delegates apportioned, elected, and governed as hereinafter provided.

Sec. 3. The State Teachers Association or Educational Association of a state, territory, or district, may become affiliated with the National Education Association and shall be designated an Affiliated State Association. Each Affiliated State Association shall be a state unit in the organization of the National Education Association and as such shall be entitled to representation in the Representative Assembly as hereinafter provided. . . .

Sec. 4. A local educational association or teachers' organization within a state, territory, or district, may affiliate with the National Education Association and shall be designated an Affiliated Local Association. Each Affiliated Local Association shall be a local unit in the organization of the National Education Association and as such shall be entitled to representation in the Representative Assembly as hereinafter provided. . . .

Sec. 6. Each Affiliated State Association shall be entitled to elect one delegate and one alternate to the Representative Assembly for each one hundred of its members or major fraction thereof, who are active members of the National Education Association, up to five hundred such active members, and thereafter one delegate and one alternate for each five hundred of its members, or major fraction thereof, who are active members of the National Education Association. Such delegates shall be designated State Delegates.

Sec. 7. Each Affiliated Local Association shall be entitled to elect one delegate and one alternate to the Representative Assembly for each one hundred of its members, or major fraction thereof, who are active members of the National Education Association. Such delegates shall be designated Local Delegates.

Sec. 8. Only active members of the National Education Association shall be eligible to be delegates to the Representative Assembly, and to vote in the election of delegates in a State or Local Affiliated Association. An active member shall be permitted to vote for the election of delegates in but one Affiliated Local Association. For determining the apportionment of delegates, an active member may be counted in two affiliated associations, and no more; and that one of these shall be the State Association.

, if only a small number of members were to participate in the policy-making sessions, business could be transacted, but action which was contrary to the wishes of the great majority might be taken, because those voting did not fairly represent anyone but themselves. Furthermore, there could be no assurance of continuity in policy in an association in which the annual business meeting was likely to vary so greatly from year to year, in size and in regional derivation as well as in personnel.

So it was natural that some form of representative control should be established. The plan adopted has corrected some of the outstanding defects of the old town-meeting government. The present body is a responsible one, with delegates elected under a systematic procedure. Their names are recorded and published, and they presumably report back to the groups that they represent. There is no longer any danger that a regional minority can control the association, for representation of near-by groups is not in proportion to attendance at the annual convention, but in proportion to membership in two associations.

There are, however, several apparent defects in the present scheme:

1. The Representative Assembly is too large. Instead of the 500 proposed by Ross as the maximum membership in a delegate body, the number of qualified delegates in attendance at the annual business meeting has ranged from a minimum of approximately 800, to 1,156 in the year 1928. It is estimated that the delegate attendance on the present basis of representation might go as high as 2,000. Clearly this number is too large for the proper functioning of a deliberative or governing body. This defect has been recognized by some of the leaders of the association, and in 1926 a Committee on the Appointment of Delegates and Kindred Questions was appointed to study the matter. This committee proposed that "the Representative Assembly shall be composed of the President and the twelve Vice-Presidents of the National Education Association and 500 delegates elected from the several states in the proportion which the number of their active members in the National Education Association bears to the total number of members of the association, provided that every state shall be entitled to at least one delegate." [9] Although this proposal was not accepted when it was submitted to the Representative Assembly in 1928, it seems certain that some such

[9] *Add. and Proc.*, 1927, p. 1031.

limitation of numbers, perhaps even more drastic than this one, will be established in the near future.

2. There is considerable overlapping of representation, due to the fact that both state and local associations elect delegates to the Representative Assembly of the National Association. The "locals" should logically be subsidiary to the state groups, and should be represented in the national body only through the state representatives. This has been proposed many times.[10] The Committee on the Appointment of Delegates and Kindred Questions, referred to above, suggested a scheme of combining each state organization with the local associations within the state into a "state unit," and dividing the state's quota of delegates between two classes in proportion to numbers, these classes being the active members of the national association who belong to an affiliated organization and the active members who do not belong to such an affiliated body; also for having the delegates from the local groups certified as state delegates.[11] This would prevent the overlapping to which objection has been made, and would at the same time remove the requirement, which has been the cause of more or less dissatisfaction, that, in order to secure representation in the assembly, a teacher is required to pay two membership fees. It is a somewhat complicated scheme, and it would undoubtedly take several years to get the machinery running smoothly so that each state would know how many delegates it should send, how many of them should be from the local affiliated groups, how many from the unaffiliated members of the National Education Association, and how these last should be elected. But from the point of view of the social engineer, it has at least some merit in that it proposes an attempt to solve immediate problems without doing violence to a complicated social structure that has been developed, by a process of integration, from many diverse smaller structures. Although it contains provisions which may cause mild conflict within the various states, especially over the apportioning of delegates between members and non-members of affiliated

---

[10] See, for example: Suzzallo, Henry, "Reorganization of the Teaching Profession," *Add. and Proc.*, 1913, pp. 362-75; Morris, Wilson C. "The American Association of Teachers," *School and Society*, VIII (Nov. 30, 1918), pp. 635-40; "Organization of the Teaching Profession," *School and Society*, IX (Jan. 25, 1919), pp. 117-18; Brainard, P. P., "First Step Toward a United Organization of Teachers," *School and Society*, XI (Feb. 21, 1920), pp. 217-20; Engelhardt, F. W., "Organization of Teachers," *School and Society*, XI (April 17, 1920), pp. 468-69; Chamberlin, Arthur H., "The Policy of the National Education Association Toward State Associations," *Add. and Proc.*, 1927, pp. 53-57.

[11] *Add. and Proc.*, 1927, pp. 1029-32.

local organizations, and between the locals on the one hand and the state association on the other, it would probably not cause so much conflict as would an attempt to arrange the various types of organizations in a logical, ascending series—local, state, and national. Eventually, after several years of discussion, and by carefully graded steps, this latter goal may be reached.

3. The membership of the Representative Assembly is not necessarily made up of those best qualified to participate in the deliberations of such a body. The practice of electing as delegates those whose travels during the summer vacation will take them near the place where the convention is to be held seems to be quite prevalent.[12] Another element in the situation, which tends to yield the same non-representative result, is that superintendents and other administrative officers commonly have their convention expenses paid in whole or in part by their boards of education, whereas classroom teachers are not thus aided out of public funds; hence, administrative officers tend to be considered available for this service while teachers are not available if the meeting is to be held at a great distance.[13] The only remedy for this situation would be the payment of the traveling expenses of all delegates out of the treasury of the associations. The National Association has appropriated various relatively small amounts for this purpose from time to time, and some of the local and state bodies have done as much in this direction as their funds would permit, to supplement what the national organization has done. But this has not yet been definitely established as a regular obligation upon the treasury and is not likely to be until the assembly is reduced in size.

4. There is too great a change in the personnel of the Representative Assembly from year to year.[14] Those who sit as first-time delegates in an assembly of more than a thousand members, an assembly that is in session for only a few hours, are not in a position to be effective representatives of anybody. Except in the cases of

[12] This statement is based on personal interviews with forty association members enrolled as graduate students at Teachers College, Columbia University. These persons came from all parts of the United States. With one exception, all reported that when the national convention is to be held at a considerable distance, a local and sometimes a state association is likely to inquire what members will be near the convention city at convention time. If any such are found, they are likely to be elected or appointed delegates.

[13] Cf. statement in Ross, *op. cit.*, p. 275: ". . . such as have the leisure and means to attend from a distance."

[14] This topic is more fully discussed in the chapter on Leadership in the present study. See also Table VI. About five-sixths of the delegates each year are "new."

the state superintendents, who are ex officio delegates, the life directors, and the constitutional officers, no continuity of participation in the assembly is assured. If the delegates' expenses were paid, and if the term were made two or three years instead of one, as at present, this defect would be removed. If, in addition, the number of delegates should be radically reduced, say to 300, the assembly would be a much more effective body, and it would be free from the possibility (perhaps, with the large body of delegates who are first-time learners, a necessity as well as a possibility) of control by a small group of "insiders," a possibility now stressed by some critics.[15]

5. Since representation is on the political-geographic basis it is probable that there are certain specialized groups of teachers in the nation who are not adequately represented, if represented at all. An editor of one of the educational periodicals, after commenting on the scant representation from the secondary field at the first meeting of the Representative Assembly in 1921, made the following suggestion:[16]

> Some plan of departmental representation might serve the double advantage of correcting the inadequacies in representation from high schools and higher institutions . . . and of uniting into a solid organization departments that tend to separate. At present, representation is on a geographic and numerical basis. Professional groups as such have no voice except through local representatives. A plan of professional representation added to the present system does not seem impossible and would have obvious advantages.

Such a scheme, if instituted, should result in a better balanced assembly, more truly representative of the teachers of the nation, not only because it would assure representation, in the assembly, of all of the present departments, but also because groups that are now organized independently would be more likely to apply for a departmental relationship if they were certain of direct representation in the general association. The one possible objection to the scheme is that it would result in further overlapping of representation in that those chosen as special group representatives would of course be likely to be members of a state association and perhaps of a local association, both of which would send a full quota of delegates of their own. This overlapping could be kept at a mini-

---

[15] "The National Education Association," *School Review*, XXXI (Sept., 1923), pp. 481-83.
[16] "The Reorganized National Education Association," *School Review*, XXIX (Sept., 1921), pp. 481-83.

mum, however, for a very small direct representation of the special groups would be all that it would be necessary to provide in order to meet the most essential requirement, namely, certainty of representation.

6. The relationship of local and state associations to the national body, referred to as "affiliation," renders the national organization relatively insecure. It depends upon nothing more than the payment of the affiliation fee each year, and of course upon the growth of the tradition of affiliation. The fact is that an indifferent attitude on the part of a few persons in a few states might seriously embarrass this immense organization in meeting its current, and certainly its long-time, obligations. If each of the state associations, if not each of the "locals," were in effect a constituent member of the national body, electing a director for the larger association [17] and delegates to the Representative Assembly, with relatively long terms and with overlapping terms, there would be much more certainty of stability.

THE DEPARTMENTS

There are within the association (1928) eighteen "departments," [18] namely:

1. The Department of Adult Education
2. The American Association of Teachers Colleges
3. The Department of Business Education
4. The Department of Classroom Teachers
5. The Department of Deans of Women
6. The Department of Elementary School Principals
7. The Department of Kindergarten-Primary Education
8. The Department of Lip Reading
9. The Department of Music Education
10. The Department of Rural Education
11. The Department of School Health and Physical Education
12. The Department of Science Instruction
13. The Department of Secondary School Principals
14. The Department of Social Studies
15. The Department of Superintendence
16. The Department of Supervisors and Directors of Instruction
17. The Department of Visual Instruction
18. The Department of Vocational Education

[17] The State Directors are chosen nominally by the full Representative Assembly, but in reality by the various state delegations acting independently.

[18] A department is an organized group of educational specialists officially recognized as a department by the association. Its meetings are announced in *The Journal* and in the convention programs, and its proceedings are published in the annual volumes of *Addresses and Proceedings*.

A new department may be established if 250 interested persons make formal application for its establishment and if two-thirds of the Board of Directors or two-thirds of the Representative Assembly approve the application at a regular meeting following the one at which the application was presented. There is the further provision that no group shall be admitted to departmental status until it has held "constructive meetings" for at least three successive years.[19]

An earlier rule provided for the establishment of a department upon application of twenty-five persons, but this was changed in 1925.

A department already in existence may be discontinued by a two-thirds vote of either the Board of Directors or of the Representative Assembly, after due announcement has been made of the proposed action. And a department is automatically discontinued if it fails to hold a regular meeting for two successive years.[20]

The departments, once established, are allowed a degree of independence. They may not admit to their own membership non-members of the National Education Association, but they may require an additional departmental membership fee to be paid, and when they do require it, they are permitted to spend all of it for their own work.[21] They may fix their own qualifications for membership, in addition to the qualification laid down by the association, namely, membership in the parent association. It is required, however, that they must admit all members of the association to their professional programs. They may hold their own meetings at a time and place different from that of the national body, if the association's Executive Committee approves. They may not establish an office outside the general headquarters of the association, unless the Executive Committee gives its consent. The secretary of each department is required to furnish the secretary of the association with a copy of the department's proceedings for publication. The number of meetings which a department may hold at the time of the convention of the parent body is limited to two, or at most to three.[22]

A general association of teachers such as the National Education Association is built fundamentally upon an assumption of common attitudes and values on the part of teachers of all levels and classes. The establishment of departments is an obvious adjustment to the

[19] By-laws, Article V, Section 8.
[20] By-laws, Article V, Section 9.
[21] By-laws, Article V, Section 9.
[22] By-laws, Article V, Section 2-7.

diversity of attitudes and values found within the membership. It is also an ·adjustment to those in the great body of teachers who are less concerned with general aspects of education than with their own specialized fields. In other words the establishment of departments has a practical, member-securing value to the association. A particular group of educational specialists is at all times faced with two choices: to organize independently, or to establish a relationship with a general association. It is to the advantage of the association to make the second course at least as attractive as the first. If an independent group becomes a "department" of the association, the membership of the association is thereby likely to be increased by the number of active members of the smaller group who have not heretofore been members of both bodies. The association gains wider contacts through the fact of becoming the promoter of a new category of educational values. It gains in social effectiveness not only because of the impression of strength created by reports of increased membership, but also because it has more values to offer when it appeals to the educational public in its campaign for new members and for attendance at its conventions. If a department does not meet at the same time as the larger body, the advantage of the relationship to the association is somewhat lessened, for it has not added to the diversity of values to be offered to those in attendance. If it were permitted to establish a separate executive office and to carry on its own work quite independently of the parent body and its program of work, the advantage would be slight, limited to the doubtful benefit coming from a "paper" alliance. The aim of the association in its rules governing its departments seems to be to make the relationship one that will be of actual value to itself.

In the case of the Department of Superintendence, the mere fact of numbers in attendance at its annual meeting would make it impracticable to hold its convention at the same time and place as that of the association itself. The very practical technological [23] matters of hotel accommodations to care for those attending the conventions, and halls large enough for the meetings, preclude the possibility of permitting this department to meet when the association meets even if it should wish to do so. And the superintendents have never wished to do so. There have been times in the past when some of their number not only favored meeting at a time different

---

[23] The reference here is to technological conditioning factors in social phenomena. See footnote 6, p. 39 of the present study.

from that of the association but actually wished to sever all connection with it.[24]

The numerical standard for the admission of a group of "interested persons"—usually specialists—to departmental status is an example of the crude adjustment which large organizations tend to make to small-group needs or desires. The professional importance of a new, specialized development cannot be determined by counting the number of "interested persons." Nor can the reciprocal value of the association and the prospective "department" be forecast in any such manner. The numerical standard is an easy one to administer, but, like all standards based on frequency and recurrence, it is a crude measure of values. Of course it may be a fairly accurate measure of association values as distinct from professional values involved in the departmental relationship. The requirement that an application for admission to such relationship must be approved by a two-thirds vote gives opportunity to the leaders not only to limit the number of such departments almost absolutely, but also to determine what kinds of specialized groups may receive departmental recognition. No group of persons, even though all are members of the association, can secure recognition as a department, with the privilege of having its meetings announced as department meetings in *The Journal* and in the convention programs and of having its proceedings printed in the annual volume of *Addresses and Proceedings*, unless it is "interested" in a phase of education or a procedure in education that is approved by this unusual majority. The additional requirement that "constructive" meetings must have been held for three years is further evidence of the great degree of control that may be exercised over the development of departments, for the right to define the word "constructive" in each instance rests with the body receiving the formal application of the group.

The departments are represented in the governing bodies of the association only indirectly. For example, they may communicate their points of view to the secretary or the president of the association, who will in turn transmit them to the Board of Directors or

[24] See p. 130. The present relationship between this department and the association, in spite of its separate meeting and its alleged feeling of superiority of a few years ago is one of very close coöperation. The paid secretary of the department serves as director of the Division of Administrative Service of the association. There is a growing tendency to speak of the meeting of the Department of Superintendence as the winter meeting of the National Education Association. Some of the other departments as well as a large number of independent organizations, more or less related in objectives to the administrative group, are now holding professional meetings at this time.

to the Representative Assembly, or they may communicate them through a member of a department who happens at the same time to be a member of one of the governing bodies.

If some scheme of departmental representation in the Representative Assembly were established, as proposed earlier in this study, groups of specialists that cannot be adequately represented under the political-geographic scheme of affiliation, and that are now organized as independent associations, might find it to their advantage to become departments of an inclusive professional body such as the National Education Association. It would be advantageous from the point of view of social economy if all specialized educational organizations could be brought into some such relationship with this association or with some other central body so that their activities might be coördinated and duplication avoided.[25]

THE EXECUTIVE STAFF

The headquarters of the association are located in Washington, D. C. At the head of the executive staff is a secretary who has general direction and oversight of the eight divisions, namely:

1. Division of Accounts
2. Legislative Division
3. Business Division
4. Division of Publications
5. Research Division
6. Division of Classroom Service
7. Division of Administrative Service (Department of Superintendence)
8. Division of Records and Membership [26]

The executive secretary is elected by the Board of Trustees for a term not to exceed four years. At the head of each division is a director who has an assistant and a staff of clerks and typists. The total number of year-round persons employed in 1928 was 100, with as many as 150 in service during certain months.

The chart (p. 37) shows the relation of the executive staff to the Representative Assembly and to the various boards, committees, and departments.

The headquarters staff is a rather highly centralized organization of paid specialists acting principally under general but sometimes under specific direction of the legislative bodies. This staff does a great and an increasing share of the actual work of the association.

[25] Ross, E. A., *op. cit.*, p. 258.
[26] Listed in the order in which they were established.

Its organization is in line with recognized administrative principles: special fitness for specialized functions; avoidance of duplication; definite placing of responsibility; authority commensurate with responsibility; relative but not absolute security. Not only are these factors of business efficiency recognized but the personnel policy seems to be such as to aim at a high morale among the staff members.[27] There is public recognition of division heads and sometimes of assistants in the annual report of the executive secretary. In their reports, heads of divisions have developed the practice of giving usually more than formal expression of appreciation for their co-workers. Frequent staff conferences deal with the whole range of problems confronting the association, thus fostering feelings of active interest in the whole enterprise rather than limiting the interest to one specialized division. It is not uncommon for the staff of one division to take over some of the work of another at times of seasonal concentration. Traditions of courtesy and consideration are apparently well established.

The executive secretary is in a relatively dominant position in the organization:

1. He may be elected for a term of four years.
2. He is elected by the five members of the Board of Trustees, four of whom are elected for terms of four years each.
3. He is the secretary of each of the principal leadership subgroups: the Representative Assembly, the Board of Directors, and the Executive Committee.
4. He has extensive authority in executive matters, the factor of geographic distance making it impractical for the Board of Directors or even for the Executive Committee to meet frequently.
5. He may exercise almost complete direction of the executive staff.
6. Members of the executive staff are assigned as consulting members of committees and commissions, and are commonly in a position to determine the methods to be used in investigations, to carry on the actual work of investigation and to organize the findings for presentation to the membership. Members of the executive staff also serve in advisory, editorial, and secretarial capacities for the various departments.
7. The mere fact of election to the position of secretary of this

[27] Ross, E. A., *op. cit.*, p. 266.

immense national association would give the one elected considerable prestige with the membership and with the leaders and with the general public. Continuing in office, becoming known through *The Journal* and other periodicals as the spokesman for the association and appearing to successive convention groups as the one most closely in touch with association problems, the executive secretary will naturally benefit by the cumulative growth of prestige.

In other words, the secretary is powerful in the organization because of a method of election and a prestige situation, each of which makes him relatively secure in his position; because of the factor of geographic distance, which prevents frequent meetings of others having constitutional authority; and because of a relationship with all the official subgroups, either directly, as an officer, or indirectly, through staff members whom he may direct. Whether he has too much power can be only a matter of opinion. Certainly the factor of geographic distance necessitates a great degree of delegated authority. The prestige situation cannot be avoided. Security of tenure could be lessened through shortening the term of office, and it could be lessened still further through transferring the right to elect this officer from the relatively permanent Board of Trustees to the constantly changing Board of Directors, or to the Representative Assembly. However, such a transfer might quickly create the danger of too little security.

The coördination of the work of the numerous subgroups is essential, and can be provided only through some kind of interlocking arrangement such as is practiced. But while there is no reason to believe that the association should take steps to reduce the dominance of the executive secretary, it should take account of this dominance by very great care in the selection of the electing body. Opening the columns of *The Journal* for free discussion of policies would provide some insurance against a misuse or misapplication of power.[28] Greater permanence in the Representative Assembly and Board of Directors through election for longer terms and through payment of expenses would result in more intelligent criticism of executive activities and policies.

The fact that there is a delegation of authority in an organization is said by Ross to indicate that the individual member does not have much at stake or that certain matters are beyond his experience

---

[28] See pp. 107-8 of the present study.

and knowledge.[29] These conditions, in addition to those just cited, may have their effect in producing the result in this association of a rather extreme delegation of authority, from the membership to the assembly, from the assembly to the Board of Directors and other smaller subgroups, with a considerable amount of power lodged finally in the executive secretary and his staff.

COMMITTEES AND COMMISSIONS

Whenever the Board of Directors or the Representative Assembly or any other subgroup becomes aware of the need of attacking some problem, it is likely to take steps to secure the creation of a committee for doing whatever needs to be done. The great variety of functions for which committees have been created during the period of this study will be adequately indicated by the selected, classified list which follows:

A. *General professional matters*
  Committee on Changes Needed in the Elementary School Course
  Committee on Character Education
  Committee on Health Problems in Education
  Committee on Thrift Education
  Committee on Visual Education
  Committee on Coördination of Research Agencies
  Committee on American Program of Education
  Committee on Ethics of the Profession
  Committee on the Teaching of Democracy
  Committee on Behavior Problem Children
  Committee on Educational Problems in Colored Schools
  Committee on Educational Coöperation Between States
  Committee on Sources of Revenue

B. *Association matters*
  Committee on Expenses of Delegates
  Editorial Council
  Committee on Revision of Departments
  Committee on Coinclusive Membership
  Committee on Appointment of Delegates and Kindred Questions
  Committee on Committees

C. *General social problems somewhat related to education*
  Committee on Foreign Educational Relations
  Committee on Child Labor
  Committee to Coöperate with American School Citizenship League
  Committee to Coöperate with Conferences on Limitation of Armaments

Committees include from one to a thousand members. The members are ordinarily appointed by the president, with the formal approval

[29] Ross, E. A., *op. cit.*, pp. 275-77.

of the Executive Committee. They are chosen sometimes from among professional acquaintances, but in the case of the larger committees, where geographic distribution is likely to be considered important, nominations are submitted by state directors, secretaries of state associations, and others. Not only is the geographic factor taken into account, but an attempt is sometimes made to include all the educational levels as well.[30]

The creation of a committee is obviously an act of adjustment to a situation in which the regularly constituted subgroups are believed to be incapable of direct or immediate or efficient functioning. It is an act of delegation of leadership in a limited area of thought or action. The need for these special subgroups may be based upon the fact that the issues involved are of a new or complex or obscure or technical character requiring more or less experience in their analysis and in the formulation of a policy; or it may be based upon the limited time at the disposal of a regularly constituted subgroup, with the consequent impossibility of giving adequate consideration to all matters. This latter condition is found in the Representative Assembly, which meets only once a year, and then for only a few hours. This body is further handicapped by being of such size that it cannot properly undertake to do more than to make a "yes" or "no" decision in complex matters. Accordingly, its usual procedure is to create special committees to study and report upon issues, with recommendation as to action to be taken, or to refer the issues to one of the smaller constitutional subgroups such as the Board of Directors or Executive Committee.

Since representation in the legislative bodies is on the political-geographic basis, the tendency to give recognition to all state groups in the membership of committees is "natural." In some cases, state representation may be relevant to the function to be performed.[31] For example, if a program which the association is promoting requires the active coöperation of state and local associations or of state legislatures, a committee to recommend a course of action would properly include representatives from all the states. But in a committee that is created for studying a general professional problem, such as the teaching of thrift, or for interpreting intricate statistical tabulations, residence within widely scattered geographic areas would seem to be almost wholly irrelevant to the

[30] According to a statement by the secretary of the association.
[31] See Ross, E. A., *op. cit.*, p. 187, for brief discussion of the "principle of relevancy."

Organization of Association 53

function to be performed. Specialized training and special study of the problem prior to the time of appointment would be among the relevant qualifications for membership in such a committee.

Furthermore, when the principle of state representation is observed in the appointment of a committee, even with provision for only one member from each state, the factor of geographic distance makes it difficult and costly for the committee to function as a unit. A common result is the delegation of most of the actual work to an active subcommittee of conveniently situated members, or to the executive staff of the association, commonly to the Division of Research. This latter tendency is not confined to committees that have a wide geographic distribution but is quite general on the part of committees that are concerned with matters involving fact-gathering, classification, and analysis. It is proper, not only because of such practical matters as expense of committee meetings, but also because fact-gathering, classification, and analysis are processes requiring technical service. Where special techniques have been established, as in these processes, it is obviously in line with social economy to make use of them instead of relying upon the common sense procedures known to ordinary members.[32]

To dispense with committees of members entirely and to have the official bodies refer all matters requiring investigation directly to the executive staff would still further add to the dominance of this staff.[33] In the interest of democratic participation and control, the wise policy would seem to be to have committees of members constantly in touch with the expert staff, determining the scope and direction of the investigation to be carried on by the staff, presenting and interpreting the report to the membership, and making recommendations as to utilization of the findings.[34]

Except in cases in which committees must be large because of the nature of their problem—as, for example, a problem requiring the coöperation of all the states and thus necessitating representation for each state—active, functional committees should be rather sharply restricted as to size. In addition to the practical reasons already noted, such as costliness of large committee meetings and difficulty in functioning as a unit, there is the additional item of decreased feeling of responsibility on the part of each member and

---

[32] Ross, E. A., *op. cit.*, p. 277.
[33] See p. 50 of the present study.
[34] Ross, E. A., *op. cit.*, p. 278.

a corresponding decrease in effectiveness. Gumplowicz, it is true, seems to disregard the matter of size and to place major emphasis upon the "common interest" among group members as determining group effectiveness, for he says: "The power of a social group increases with the number of common interests among its members, irrespective of size."[35] Yet he declares: "The number of common interests varies inversely with the number of individuals in the social group."[36]

Great size is, however, relevant to one function which committees may perform, namely, securing the attention of the general public and perhaps influencing public opinion as to an issue to which the association is already committed. A committee of one hundred or one thousand is certainly not likely to be efficient in investigation and in analysis and in formulation of recommendations—the typical activities of most committees—but the very fact of size guarantees it a wide public hearing. As Ross puts it, such a committee becomes a sounding board.[37] The creation of committees of enormous size may then under certain conditions be not only entirely proper but extremely valuable to the association as a propaganda technique. It must be evident that the committee's prestige and its resultant usefulness to the group will be due not only to the fact of its size, but to the personal prestige of its own leaders and members.

THE NATIONAL COUNCIL OF EDUCATION

The by-laws of the association (Article IV, Sections 1-3) provide for the creation of this council as follows:[38]

Section 1. The National Council of Education shall discuss educational questions of public and professional interest; propose to the Executive Committee, from time to time, suitable subjects for investigation and research; have a report made at its annual meeting on "Educational Progress During the Past Year"; and in other ways use its best efforts to further the objects of the association and to promote the cause of education in general.

Sec. 2. The National Council of Education shall consist of one hundred twenty regular members, selected from the active membership of the National Education Association. Any active member of the association is eligible to membership in the Council and each member shall be elected for six years and until his successor is elected. In addition to the 120 members thus selected from the active membership, the National Council may in its by-

---

[35] As quoted by P. P. Jacobs, *German Sociology*, p. 65.
[36] *Ibid.*, p. 65. Cf. Spykman, N. J., *The Social Theory of Georg Simmel*, p. 136.
[37] Ross, E. A., *op. cit.*, p. 276.
[38] *Add. and Proc.*, 1928, pp. 1025-26.

laws provide for the admission to membership of representatives from the several departments of the association on the basis of equal representation from each department.[39]

Sec. 3. The annual election of members of the Council shall be held at the time of the annual meeting of the association. The Board of Directors of the association shall annually elect ten members and the Council ten members, and each body shall fill all vacancies in its quota of members. No state, territory, nor district in the United States shall have at one time more than seven regular members in the Council.

The council is thus seen to be a body having no active directive or legislative function. It exists for the purpose of general discussion and for the purpose of advising the active leaders of the association as to "suitable subjects for investigation and research" and as to various general matters.

Sharp limitation of membership, added to the implication contained in the by-laws that this subgroup is competent to assume an advisory rôle in its relationship to the active leadership of the association, would tend to give such a body as the National Council great prestige with the members of the association and would tend to give the council itself a definite consciousness of its own prestige. However, this prestige is all that it has to rely upon in its control of any of the activities of the association, for it can only *"propose suitable subjects for investigation and research . . . and use its best efforts* to further the objects of the association and to promote the cause of education in general." It cannot give directions. Moreover, the Executive Committee, the leadership subgroup to which the council's proposals may be made, is itself a body with great prestige in the association and with a consciousness of its own prestige. It is likely to feel itself fully as competent to determine current activities as is the council. Besides, this committee is directly responsible to the association as a whole for the activities of a particular year, with a very large share of the responsibility borne inescapably by the president of the association, whereas the council cannot be held responsible for anything. Under these conditions, it is not surprising to find that the council has little direct influence upon the policies of the association. Its influence is probably not greater than is that of a similar number of leaders in education meeting entirely independently of the national association. In other words, its influence is indirect. It may properly be described as a learned society established by the National Education

---

[39] The active membership now includes three chosen from each of the departments.

Association from its membership. Obviously, it has values from a general professional point of view, but there is nothing in the record and there is nothing in the social situation to indicate that a practical service is rendered directly to the association.

CHAPTER IV

THE ACTIVE RESPONSIBLE LEADERSHIP OF THE ASSOCIATION

"Not all individuals," says Professor Giddings, "react to a given stimulation with equal promptness, completeness, or persistence. Therefore, in every situation there are individuals that react more effectively than others do. They reinforce the original stimulation and play a major part in interstimulation. They initiate and take responsibility. They lead. . . ."[1] They not only "react more effectively" but in their reactions they either express what the others feel and believe or else they have the ability to make group attitudes conform to their own. Their suggestions seem "to embrace what is best in the views of others and to embody the inevitable conclusion."[2] These are the "natural" leaders of publics, crowds, movements, and casual groups.[3] They do not require formal election to a leadership status. They are "naturally" followed by their fellows.

In organized groups, on the other hand, leaders are formally chosen. The tendency would be for the formal process of election to result in establishing in positions of group leadership those that would be elevated to such status by the natural selective processes, for these processes are operating just as certainly in organized as in unorganized groups.

Obviously, in a large, complex organization such as the National Education Association, leadership is multiple. The group engages in a variety of activities, under a variety of conditions. A member who has the requisite qualities for acting on behalf of the group in one situation may not be acceptable to the group in another situation. One who has the "personality-prestige"[4] to enable him to lead in general policy-making or executive activities may not have

---

[1] Giddings. F. H., *Studies in the Theory of Human Society*, pp. 267-68
[2] Cooley, C. H., *Human Nature and the Social Order*, pp. 328-31.
Allport, F. H., *Social Psychology*, pp. 420-21.
[3] Kulp, D. H., II, *Outlines of the Sociology of Human Behavior*, Chaps. XXXIII and XXXIV.
[4] Allport, F. H., *op. cit.*, pp. 420-21.

the specialized training needed for leadership in technical matters.[5] The expectation would be that leadership functions would be delegated to numerous individual leaders and leadership groups and subgroups, all chosen directly or indirectly by the members on bases relevant to the functions to be performed.

The active, responsible leadership of this association includes the officers, the Board of Trustees, the Executive Committee, the Board of Directors, the committees, the Representative Assembly, and the executive (headquarters) staff.[6] The aim in the present chapter is to analyze these leadership subgroups, as objectively as possible, for the period under discussion. The data are not complete. No data are available, for example, as to the ages of the leaders, their general and technical training, the length of their service in the professional field of education, or their "personality-prestige." Concerning certain other characteristics, however, objective data, namely, those concerning sex, educational position, and continuity of service in association leadership are available and are here presented and analyzed. After each class of data has been presented separately, the inter-relationships of the three classes are shown.

[5] Cf. Smith, W. R., *Principles of Educational Sociology,* pp. 66-68.

[6] The National Council of Education is not included because it is not directly concerned with active, responsible leadership functions in the association. It is true that the general description of its intended functions, as found in the By-laws (Article IV, Section 1) seems to charge it with leadership responsibility, for its purposes are said to be: discussion, proposing subjects for investigation, reporting on educational progress, furthering the objects of the association, and promoting the cause of education. As it is actually functioning, it may be quite accurately described as a partially self-perpetuating learned society, created by the association from its membership. (See pp. 55-56.) Its leadership is not specifically focused upon the National Education Association but is a general professional leadership. It does not plan meetings of association members; it does not take part, as a group, in policy-making discussions of the association; it does not have any responsibility for financial management activities or expansion efforts or legislative programs of the association. It neither gives directions to the association nor receives directions from it. The Bureau of Education Bulletin entitled *A Handbook of Educational Associations* and *Foundations in the United States* (Bull. 1926, No. 16) gives quite an accurate statement of the character of this organization when it reports its purpose as follows: "To reach and disseminate correct thinking on educational questions and to define and state with accuracy the different views and theories, with reason for each."

However, even though the Council is not included among the active responsible leadership groups, it is of interest to note that in sex composition, it does not differ materially from the leadership groups, there being in the elected membership of the Council in 1928, eighty-six men and thirty-four women. The distribution of educational positions is somewhat different from that in the other groups, there being relatively more of the college-university-teachers college class and fewer superintendents and state school authorities. This same 1928 group, excluding the members chosen by the departments, is distributed among the eight classes of Table III as follows: Class 1, eleven; Class 2, twenty-six; Class 3, six; Class 4, thirty-seven; Class 5, three; Class 6, one; Class 7, nineteen, and Class 8, seventeen.

SEX DISTRIBUTION

Under an unwritten agreement, the presidency of the association alternates between the sexes. This means that the position of first vice-president alternates also, for this position is held by the retiring president.[7] As to the other places of leadership, there is apparently no agreement. In Tables I and II the sex composition of all the association and department leadership subgroups is shown. Ex officio membership, as for example, the membership of the president of the Board of Trustees, is not counted, since to count it would be to include it twice. Sex was determined by given names. Where only initials were recorded the persons were counted as males.[8]

TABLE I

Sex Distribution in Offices and in Leadership Subgroups of the National Education Association, 1918 to 1928, in Service-Years

Position	Men		Women		Total
	Number	Per Cent	Number	Per Cent	Number
President	5	45.5	6	54.5	11
First vice-president	6	54.5	5	45.5	11
Second and other vice-presidents	76	63.9	43	36.1	119
Treasurer	6	54.5	5	45.5	11
Board of Trustees (elected members)	31	70.5	13	29.5	44
Executive committee (elected member)	7	63.6	4	36.4	11
State directors	479	81.9	106	18.1	585
Committees*	2,520	62.3	1,525	37.7	4,045
Representative assembly: 1926, 1927, 1928	1,423	41.3	2,024	58.7	3,447
Average of percentages†		59.8		40.2	

* Committees for 1918, 1919, 1920, 1923, and 1924, and Representative Assembly prior to 1926 not included because records were incomplete.
† Column totals and percentages based on these totals are omitted for the reason that not all the data are for the same number of years.

The secretary of the association states[9] that in many instances when attempts are made to place women on committees and in other

[7] By-laws, Article III, Section 1.
[8] There is a possibility of a slight margin of error in the assumption that only men use their initials in filling out membership cards and other credentials. However, a complete check (by personal letters) of the ninety Minnesota, Wisconsin, Iowa, North Dakota, and South Dakota delegates for whom initials were used in the 1926, 1927, and 1928 records showed that all were men. It is felt, therefore, that the error in the assumption is so slight that it may be safely disregarded for all practical purposes.
[9] Personal communication.

TABLE II

Sex Distribution in Offices of Departments of the National Education Association, 1918 to 1928

Office	Men		Women		Total
	Number	Per Cent	Number	Per Cent	Number
President.......................	136	69.0	61	31.0	197
Vice-president...................	113	60.1	75	39.9	188
Secretary, treasurer, secretary-treasurer, librarian.............	95	42.8	127	57.2	222
Members of executive committee....	84	67.2	41	32.8	125
Total......................	428	58.5	304	41.5	732

positions of leadership in the association, they refuse to serve. The social tradition which causes male leadership to be considered "natural"; the possibility of having to expend money from a rather moderate income; relative lack of flexibility in work schedule on the part of women, who are mainly classroom teachers, as compared with men, many of whom are administrators—these are among the factors tending to produce sex inequality in the leadership of the association.[10]

EDUCATIONAL POSITIONS OF LEADERS

Members of the leadership subgroups were classified on the basis of educational positions held. The results of this classification are shown in Table III.

The members of the Representative Assembly are classified separately in Table IV, using the records for only 1926, 1927, and 1928, for the reason that for the other years the educational position was not indicated in a sufficiently large percentage of cases to make a classification significant. In the relatively few cases in which the record for these last three years does not show the educational positions of the elected delegates, they have been counted as teachers. The ex officio delegates, that is, the constitutional officers of the as-

---

[10] Although the leadership of departments is not the leadership of the association, it will be of interest to compare sex distribution in the departmental offices now with what Alexander found in 1909-1910. He reports that of fifty-seven offices, women held two presidencies, these in departments composed entirely of women; five vice-presidencies, "purely honorary positions"; and seven secretaryships, "not generally counted places of any great importance" (Appendix, pp. 173 ff.). Table II shows the sex distribution in various departmental offices from 1918 to 1928.

TABLE III
Leaders of the Association, 1918 to 1928, Classified by Educational Position, in Service-Years

Office	President Number	President Per Cent	First Vice-President Number	First Vice-President Per Cent	Second and Other Vice-Presidents Number	Second and Other Vice-Presidents Per Cent	Treasurer Number	Treasurer Per Cent	Board of Trustees (Elected Members) Number	Board of Trustees (Elected Members) Per Cent	Executive Committee (Elected Member) Number	Executive Committee (Elected Member) Per Cent	State Directors Number	State Directors Per Cent	Committees* Number	Committees* Per Cent	Average of Percentages, All Columns	Averages of Percentages, Four Most Numerous Offices †
State superintendents or commissioners of education, their deputies, assistants, inspectors, examiners, directors	3	27.3	3	27.3	33	27.7			1	2.3	3	27.3	142	24.3	309	7.6	18.0	15.5
City and county superintendents or commissioners, their deputies and assistants	3	27.3	3	27.3	37	31.1	6	54.5	14	31.8	1	9.1	177	30.3	986	24.4	22.7	29.4
Principals	2	18.2	2	18.2	10	8.4	5	45.5	2	4.5			44	7.5	427	10.6	8.4	7.8
Presidents, deans, or other officers of teachers colleges, colleges, and universities	1	9.1	2	18.2	16	13.4			6	13.6	1	9.1	82	14.0	561	13.9	18.2	13.7
Teachers	2	18.2	1	9.1	7	5.9			9	20.5	1	9.1	20	3.4	253	6.3	14.8	9.0
Secretaries of state teachers' associations					1	0.8							44	7.5	123	3.0	1.4	2.8
Educational position not shown in record					10	8.4			4	9.1	4	36.4	62	10.6	826	20.4	10.6	12.1
Miscellaneous positions not classified in first six categories					5	4.2			8	18.2	1	9.1	14	2.4	560	13.8	6.0	9.7
Total	11	100	11	100	119	100	11	100	44	100	11	100	585	100	4045	100	100	100

* Committees for 1918, 1919, 1920, 1923, and 1924 not included because records were not complete.
† Eliminating offices of president, first vice-president, treasurer, and executive committee member, in which numbers are too small to show any general tendency.

TABLE IV

MEMBERS OF REPRESENTATIVE ASSEMBLY FOR 1926, 1927, AND 1928, CLASSIFIED BY EDUCATIONAL POSITION AND BY OFFICIAL RELATIONSHIP TO THE ASSOCIATION*

Position	Number	Per Cent
State superintendents and commissioners, their deputies, assistants, inspectors, examiners, directors.................	93	2.69
City and county superintendents, their deputies, etc..........	620	17.97
Principals..	487	14.13
Presidents, deans, professors in colleges, universities, teachers colleges...	66	1.92
Teachers...	1,970	57.15
Secretaries of state teachers' associations...................	66	1.92
Vice-presidents, secretary, treasurer, executive committee, Board of Trustees, of National Education Association.......	18	0.52
State directors...	101	2.93
Past presidents, life directors..............................	19	0.55
Miscellaneous: board of education members, editor, clerk.......	7	0.20
Total...	3,447	100.00

* Total ex officio membership represented in this table is 227 (6.59 per cent).

sociation, state superintendents and commissioners of education [11] and past presidents of the association are classified in the annual records on the basis of their relationship to the association rather than as to their professional position. This is of significance in this study because of its bearing on the problem of the propriety of permitting ex officio representation—a problem upon which there has been open disagreement within the association from time to time.

CONTINUITY OF SERVICE

It is of importance to discover whether or not leaders, once selected, continue to serve for a considerable time, or whether there is frequent change. Continuity of service on the Board of Trustees is provided in the charter, which fixes the term of the four elected members of this board as four years. The secretary of the association is elected by the trustees for a term "not to exceed four years." The president is elected for a one-year term, but he automatically becomes first vice-president for the year following, and in the latter office is in a position to continue to exercise considerable influence upon the organization. The year-round members of the headquarters staff, with the exception of the secretary of the association, are

[11] By-laws, Article II, Section 9.

on indefinite tenure.[12] With these exceptions, the leaders are chosen for one year. It is true that committees may continue to serve for a much longer period than one year, and frequently the full membership will be reappointed year after year, but the president may change the entire personnel if he wishes to do so. There is a definite tendency to reëlect the treasurer and trustees over and over again. There is much less continuity of service on the part of the elected member of the Executive Committee, there having been only two reelections in the eleven years included in the present study, and these having been for only a one-year extension. The positions of second and lower vice-presidents are almost entirely honorary in character, so there is no reason why they should not be "passed around" as much as possible, and this is actually done. Continuity of service on the part of state directors is shown in Table V.

TABLE V

CONTINUITY OF SERVICE OF STATE DIRECTORS OF THE NATIONAL EDUCATION ASSOCIATION, 1918 TO 1928*†

Year	Number of State Directors	Serving Second Year		Serving Third Year		Serving Fourth Year	
		Number	Per Cent	Number	Per Cent	Number	Per Cent
1918	53	30	56.6	18	34.0	12	22.6
1919	53	25	47.2	14	26.4	9	17.0
1920	52	24	46.2	16	30.8	11	21.2
1921	52	29	55.8	20	38.5	12	23.1
1922	53	29	54.7	18	34.0	13	24.5
1923	53	31	58.5	26	49.1	16	30.2
1924	54	40	74.1	24	44.4	14	25.9
1925	54	32	59.3	21	38.9	10	18.5
1926	54	34	63.0	19	35.2	...	...
1927	54	29	53.7	...	...	...	...
Average	53.2	30.3	56.9	19.6	36.8	12.1	22.8

* Range in length of term, from one to nine years. Number serving nine years, 5; eight years, 4; seven years, 2; six years, 5; five years, 8; four years, 19; three years, 29; two years, 52; one year, 158; average length of term, 1.92 years.
† This table is to be read as follows: Of the 53 persons serving as state directors in 1918, 30 (56.6 per cent) were still serving in 1919, 18 (34 per cent) in 1920, and 12 (22.6 per cent) in 1921.

The Board of Directors is made up not only of state directors, who are elected annually, but it includes also a number of life direc-

[12] The conditions seem to be of a kind to produce long tenure in these positions. The secretary of the association has served continuously during the period of this study. All present heads of divisions have served continuously since 1918, or since their divisions were created, with two exceptions, and in these two cases there has been no change since 1923.

tors: (1) former presidents of the association, (2) United States Commissioners of Education, and (3) certain persons and institutions that paid life membership fees under an old rule of the association in the 1880's. The number of life directors has not been greater than twenty-seven, at least not in recent years, and not many of them take an active part in the meetings of the Board of Directors. For example, at the seven meetings of the board in February and July, 1928, the total attendance varied from thirty-six to fifty-nine, and the attendance of life directors from four to eleven.

Because of the large numbers involved, it was not considered feasible to make a complete enumeration of persons serving more than one year in the Representative Assembly. Moreover, the names of delegates were omitted from the 1923 records. Since it is necessary to have a continuous record in order to have any basis for conclusions as to continuity of service, this phase of the study has been limited to the years 1924 to 1928. Seven states that were believed to be fairly typical (Connecticut, Pennsylvania, Indiana, Colorado, Oregon, Texas, North Carolina) were studied, and the record of the continuity of their delegates' service during the limited period is to be found in Table VI. In making this selection of states the two factors of geographic situation and density of population were taken into account.

TABLE VI

CONTINUITY OF MEMBERSHIP IN THE REPRESENTATIVE ASSEMBLY OF THE NATIONAL EDUCATION ASSOCIATION FROM CERTAIN SELECTED STATES, 1924 TO 1928*

Year	Number of Delegates	Serving Second Year		Serving Third Year	
		Number	Per Cent	Number	Per Cent
1924............	172	25	14.5	22	12.8
1925............	182	29	15.9	22	12.1
1926............	211	34	16.1	25	11.8
1927............	199	41	20.6	...	....
Total......	764	129	16.9	69†	12.2

* This table is to be read as follows: Of the 172 persons serving as delegates in 1924, 25 (14.5 per cent) returned as delegates in 1925, and 22 (12.8 per cent) in 1926.
† Out of a total of 565 two years earlier.

It will be noted that of the 764 delegates, only 129 returned to serve a second year. Of this number (129) seventeen were delegates ex officio: state superintendents, state directors, and past presidents. Of the remainder, forty-seven were classified as teachers, thirty as superintendents and supervisors, sixteen as principals, eleven as presidents and deans, and eight as secretaries of state associations. Of the total of 565 for 1924, 1925, and 1926, sixty-nine were found to be delegates two years later. Of these, six were delegates ex officio, twenty-two were superintendents and supervisors, eighteen were teachers, ten were secretaries of state associations, nine were principals, and four were presidents and deans.

A study of continuity of service in committees is obviously limited to committees that continue for more than one year. This eliminates convention committees and many special committees. For several reasons it is difficult to handle the figures for the longer-lived committees in any significant way. Up to 1921, the records of committee membership are incomplete. From 1922 to 1928, the records are apparently complete, but the situation is complicated by the fact that the size of committees was being increased from 1924 and 1925 on. In the presence of a new policy as to committee size, it is impossible to reach any conclusion as to whether or not persons who were reappointed to service in an enlarged committee would have been continued in service if the committee had remained of the original size. Moreover, membership in a large committee is usually to be interpreted as filling a "sounding-board" or prestige function [13] rather than an active leadership function, so that, no matter what the figures might show as to continuity of committee membership, the figures for the larger committees would not necessarily have meaning as to continuity of leadership. In the case of the smaller committees, however, an active leadership function is likely to be involved, namely, to point the way in a situation that is new or complex or obscure or technical.[14] An example of a committee of this kind is the Committee on Health Problems in Education. From 1922 to 1928 its size was changed only slightly. It had the same chairman throughout the entire period. Of the sixteen members in 1922, fourteen were still included in 1923, thirteen in 1924, twelve in 1925, nine in 1926, nine in 1927, and eight in 1928. Another committee in which the continuity of service of the 1922 members has been notable is the Legislative Commission. Of the twelve members in 1922, ten were listed as members in 1923, ten in 1924, ten in 1925, ten in 1926, six in 1927, and seven in 1928. However, this

[13] See pp. 53-54 of the present study.
[14] See p. 52 of the present study.

record has little meaning as compared with that of the Committee on Health Problems, in which the total membership changed very little (twenty being the maximum) while the size of the Legislative Commission was increased to 101 in 1927 and to 129 in 1928.

If we take the seven committees that continued in existence through the three-year period, 1926 to 1928, the record of continuity of service is as shown in Table VII. It is impossible to draw any conclusions as to continuity of committee membership from this table.

TABLE VII

CONTINUITY OF MEMBERSHIP IN COMMITTEES OF THE NATIONAL EDUCATION ASSOCIATION, 1926 TO 1928*

Year	Members	Serving Second Year		Serving Third Year	
		Number	Per Cent	Number	Per Cent
1926...........	370	148	40.0	151	40.8
1927...........	516	471	91.3	...	...

* This table is to be read as follows: Of the 370 persons serving as committee members in 1926, 148 (40 per cent) continued as members in 1927, and 159 (40.8 per cent) in 1928.

As just pointed out, the size of committees was being increased. Probably the inactive members, including some of those who under another policy as to increased size would have been dropped from the list, were permitted to remain on the roll. This policy no doubt accounts for the fact that 471 of the original 516 were still listed a year after the publication of names of members in 1927, and for the further fact that in 1928 some who had dropped out were apparently reappointed to the 1926 committees.

ANALYSIS OF LEADERSHIP DATA

Sex Distribution. Although there are probably four or five times as many women as there are men in the National Education Association, the leadership of the association is predominantly male, men outnumbering women approximately in the ratio of three to two. The proportion of women is, however, strikingly greater than that reported in Alexander's study in 1910.[15] The only leadership group in which women predominate is the Representative Assembly, and in that group there are approximately three women to every two men. Through their voting strength in this body, women could,

[15] See pp. 173-76 of the present study.

if the sex representation issue were sharply drawn at any time, actually take possession of all the offices. The fact that they do not do so is evidence that the issue is not of primary importance in the minds of a considerable number of the women representatives.

However, a factor affecting the power of women representatives in this matter of offices, or in any other matter where the sex element might be considered, is the factor of continuity of service, as reported in Table VI and on page 64. Among the few delegates who return for a second or third year of service, there is only one teacher to every two or three in the other classes combined, which is approximately the same as saying that there is one woman to every two or three men in the group of experienced leaders in the assembly. Concerted action on the part of six or seven hundred women members, more than five-sixths of whom are serving their first year as delegates, would be very difficult to achieve during the few days when the convention is in session even if most of them wished to achieve it.

At present there is no evidence that in the election of leaders the sex representation issue is alive except the unrecorded "gentlemen's agreement" that the presidency shall alternate between the sexes. This agreement is gathering, through unbroken observance, the cumulative strength of a tradition.

As to the other positions, it seems probable that they will continue to be filled more largely by men than by women, for the following reasons:

1. Men are more numerous than women in the educational administrative field, a field in which leadership of teaching staffs is involved, hence they are likely to be considered more competent in leadership in that they have had experience in leadership in their professional positions.
2. Administrators are likely to be considered more available for duties in the association in that they are more free than classroom teachers to travel on association business during the school year, both because of the nature of their work with its relatively flexible time schedule and because many of them are able to have their traveling expenses paid from public funds.
3. The professional levels on which practically all the men engaged in education are working—college teaching, administration, high school teaching—are more "looked up to" than are those occupied almost exclusively by women—elementary

teaching and rural teaching.[16] This would tend to give the male members of the association something of an advantage in the matter of office holding.

4. There is a traditional element of "sex spacing" which tends to operate to place men in important positions, irrespective of factors of age, position, training, experience, and personal fitness.[17] In other words, the same social attitudes which place men in positions of responsibility in the schools will place them in positions of responsibility in the association.

Educational Positions of Leaders. There is no classification available of the membership of the National Education Association on the basis of educational position. Consequently it is impossible to determine how nearly proportional is the representation of each of the occupational subgroups in the leadership subgroups. Just as we would be relatively certain that men would hold more than their proportionate share of the offices, for reasons just pointed out, so we should expect that the professional groups which are predominantly male would have more than their share of the leadership positions. And this is convincingly shown to be the case in Tables III and IV. The position of president, and consequently that of first vice-president, has been rather well "passed around," although there is no evidence of a plan to secure this result. Numbers involved in these offices, as well as in those of treasurer and elected member of the Executive Committee are too small to indicate any general tendency. In other offices, however—those of second and lower vice-presidents, members of Board of Trustees, state directors, and committee members—the tendency is clear. City and county superintendents rank first in all of these positions, being almost twice as numerous as the next class, members of state departments of education. If we eliminate the last two classes in Table III, that is, "Educational position not shown in record" and "Miscellaneous," members of faculties of higher institutions are third in rank, "teachers" are fourth, principals fifth, and secretaries of state teachers' associations a poor sixth.

Table IV embodies conclusive evidence that if teachers desired to fill all the offices and leadership subgroups with members of their

---

[16] Cf. Count, George S., "The Social Status of Occupations," *School Review*, XXXIII (Jan., 1925), pp. 16-27.

[17] Cf. Ross, E. A., *Principles of Sociology*, pp. 255-56; Allport, F. H., *Social Psychology*, p. 249.

own class, they could do so, for they have more than 57 per cent of the voting strength in the Representative Assembly. That they have not done so is to be interpreted as due to almost precisely the same factors that influence the sex distribution, namely:

1. Lack of special class consciousness or conflict consciousness (teachers *vs.* administrators and others) on the part of at least some teachers.
2. Large turnover in the membership of the Representative Assembly from year to year, larger among those classified as teachers than among the other classes, resulting in lack of organizability for concerted action, even though such action was desired by teachers quite generally.
3. Familiarity with the customary school situation in which leadership is legally delegated to administrators.
4. The very practical matters of expense and inflexible work schedule—these limiting teachers more than they limit the members of the other classes in their acceptance of office-holding obligations.
5. The lower social recognition given to teachers. Teachers are not so much "looked up to" even by themselves as are the others.
6. The traditional acceptance of male leadership, there being relatively fewer men classified as teachers than as state, city, and county superintendents, officers in higher institutions of learning, principals, and secretaries of state associations.

The ex officio representation in the Representative Assembly was at one time believed by some members to be likely to monopolize leadership functions, in other words to dominate the association.[18] State superintendents and commissioners seem to have been especially feared. They seem not to have been very active, however. What the total ex officio membership (6.59 per cent of the total membership as shown in Table IV) could do by way of controlling the assembly, only 16.9 per cent of whose members return for a second year and only 12.2 per cent for a third year,[19] can be only a matter of conjecture. The prestige [20] of the state officers would certainly render this small group very powerful in its influence upon an in-

---

[18] See p. 129 of the present study.
[19] Table VI.
[20] Cf. Hayes, E. C., *Introduction to the Study of Sociology*, p. 324: "The prestige of place or of the official class."

experienced assembly. The problems connected with other ex officio members, namely, the constitutional officers of the association and the past presidents, who are life directors, can be discussed more properly under the head of continuity of service.

Continuity of Service. The significance of the factor of continuity of leadership rests on two assumptions:

1. Long terms in office in any organization are likely to result in stabilized, consistent policy, whereas short terms mean an absence of predictability as to policy from year to year.[21]
2. Long terms involve uncertainty as to quick responsiveness to democratic control, while short terms mean relative certainty that the "will" of the members will find accurate expression.[22]

Inspection of the provisions of the constitution and by-laws would lead to the conclusion that constant adjustment to democratic control is assured, even at the cost of danger to consistency and stability in policy, except in the case of the Board of Trustees, for this is the only group of leaders of whom a majority are elected for more than one year. Moreover, no constitutional officer is necessarily chosen for more than a one-year term, although the secretary *may* be—and actually has been—elected for a term as long as four years, and the retiring president automatically serves as first vice-president for a year. There is no assurance that at a particular time any Executive Committee member except the first vice-president will have had previous experience in the business of the association, and even to this officer these responsibilities may have been new a year earlier.

Consistency and stability might be insured, in the absence of provision for long terms on the part of leaders, by the practice of re-electing officers and delegates for a succession of terms. The extent to which this practice is followed in electing state directors and Representative Assembly delegates is shown in Tables V and VI. Approximately half the elected members of the Board of Directors return for a second year, and about one-third for a third year. In the assembly only about one-sixth of the delegates at any annual meeting are serving their second term, and only about one-eighth their third term. It appears, therefore, that on the basis of the assumptions made, consistency and stability are likely to be found in the policies adopted by the Board of Directors for at least two years in succession, especially since there are several life directors

[21] Ross, E. A., *op. cit.*, pp. 271-72.
[22] Ogg, F. A. and Ray, P. O., *Introduction to American Government*, pp. 355-56.

Responsible Leadership 71

who are likely to be influential in continuing old policies. In the Representative Assembly, however, on the basis of members returning for more than one session, there can be absolutely no prediction that the policy of a particular year will be like that of the last or the next. Other factors in the situation besides numbers, however, promote stability and consistency even in the assembly.

1. There is the somewhat permanent membership of state superintendents and commissioners of education. The prestige of this official class is such that these persons would exercise an influence entirely out of proportion to their number.
2. The policy of some affiliated associations evidently is to elect delegates for more than one term. The influence of these experienced delegates upon the great numbers of new delegates in these large gatherings held during a period of only three or four days would be out of proportion to their numbers. The factor of experience conditions the one class for active leadership and that of inexperience conditions the other for "followership." [23]
3. There is the additional fact that most of the experienced delegates are men. This would tend to increase their relative influence in the affairs of the association.
4. Most of the experienced delegates are administrators or members of other educational classes having more than ordinary social recognition. This would have an effect in the same direction as the preceding factor, that is, it would tend to increase the power of this experienced minority.

It may be said, then, that although there are short terms in office for the great majority of the members of the assembly, this fact does not necessarily indicate anything as to the assembly's responsiveness to the "will" of the members of the association, nor as to the likelihood of consistent and stable policy. Evidence upon the latter point will be found in Chapter V.

[23] Ross, E. A., *op. cit.*, pp. 255-56.

CHAPTER V

ACTIVITIES AND OBJECTIVES OF THE ASSOCIATION

What does a group actually do? Why does it engage in particular activities? These are questions of a fundamental character in the study of any group. The present chapter and Chapters VI and VII are devoted to a detailed description and analysis of the activities of this association as a whole and of its official leadership groups and subgroups, together with a consideration of the conditions under which these activities are carried on. The general basis for classification, so far as the activities may be classified, is that of *intended function*.

THE ANNUAL CONVENTION

One of the most conspicuous activities of the organization is the holding of an annual convention in the summer. This is likely to attract as many as 10,000 teachers if it is held in the East or Middle West. After a religious or semi-religious meeting on Sunday, the first formal session of the convention is customarily held on Monday. Meetings continue from then until Friday, general sessions in the forenoons and evenings and departmental sessions in the afternoons. At each session, one or more persons read or deliver prepared addresses on topics announced several weeks beforehand in *The Journal* and listed also in separate form as an official program to be distributed to those in actual attendance at the convention. The Representative Assembly holds its meetings while some of the general sessions are in progress.

Addresses at General Sessions. The program for the general sessions is arranged by the president of the association with the active aid of the executive secretary and his staff. This program was one of the major values of membership in the association before its reorganization, and there can be no doubt that it still is for those who live relatively near the convention city.

With what kinds of topics does the association deal in these public programs? What do the leaders and the speakers intend to be the values achieved through these addresses? At what do they aim?

Activities and Objectives

In an attempt to answer these questions, an analysis has been made of the 349 papers and addresses given at the general sessions during the period covered by this study.[1] The results of this analysis are to be found in Table VIII, counting each paper or address as a unit of communication.

TABLE VIII

ADDRESSES AT GENERAL SESSIONS OF THE NATIONAL EDUCATION ASSOCIATION ANNUAL CONVENTIONS, 1918 TO 1928, CLASSIFIED UNDER DEFINED CATEGORIES

Category	1918	1919	1920	1921	1922	1923	1924	1925	1926	1927	1928	Total	Per Cent
Interpretation.......	5	3	2	..	5	1	4	2	6	5	2	35	10.0
Inspiration..........	4	..	..	1	2	1	8	2	3	2	2	25	7.2
Stimulation.........	2	1	4	1	3	10	3	1	2	..	..	27	7.7
Educational information.............	2	..	4	..	1	3	1	4	4	..	6	25	7.2
General information..	7	..	2	1	2	2	..	6	1	1	5	27	7.7
Discussion of affairs of collective group....	2	2	4	1	1	..	..	6	1	7	1	25	7.2
Discussion of matters affecting welfare of members..........	1	..	1	..	..	..	..	..	..	5	..	7	2.0
Communication of subgroup points of view.............	2	8	9	18	..	..	4	10	5	10	5	71	20.3
Communication from outside groups.....	4	10	..	1	3	4	1	2	7	..	3	35	10.0
General and educational philosophy...	5	..	6	..	5	1	1	2	6	2	2	30	8.6
Formal expressions...	3	5	3	3	1	4	2	3	5	6	7	42	12.0
Total..........	37	29	35	26	23	26	24	38	40	38	33	349	100.0

The eleven categories used are defined as follows:

I. *Interpretation.* Defining, apparently for the new and uninformed in the group, and indirectly for other groups, by a member who assumes to speak for the group, of practices, points of view, relationships, standards, objectives, which the group has implicitly or explicitly adopted with respect to education, the school, and the association itself.

Case illustration: The new world in which we live has added in manifold ways to the objectives of education. Education means to-day a preparation for living according to the highest standards of this age. It differs from the

---

[1] As reprinted in full or in abridged form in the annual volume of *Addresses and Proceedings of the National Education Association.* Many of the addresses are printed as abstracts or summaries. These abstracts had been either prepared or approved by the speakers themselves. (*Add. and Proc.,* 1921, pp. vi, 237.)

older education as modern life for which it is a preparation. If more emphasis is laid upon vocational, industrial, and practical business education to-day than formerly, it is because it is an age of new vocations, industrial expansion, and business opportunity. If education for life in a democracy has essential differences from education for life under older and less liberal forms of government, it is because it reflects a larger participation on the part of the citizen in the affairs of government and a greater political right and responsibility; if education is more complicated and more exacting than formerly, it is because modern life is more complex and its needs correspondingly multiplied and varied, and because modern invention has made the world a neighborhood.

The exigencies of modern life with its variety of complex problems make new and greater demands upon the individual for mental and physical preparation. New crises are ever disclosing old weaknesses and unfolding new demands and possibilities. Education, therefore, must be evolutionary and plastic. It must be sensitive to changing needs, but must never be decoyed from its path by wanton caprice or passing fads.

The objectives of education in America at present are comparatively simple and well defined though plans for their accomplishment are not uniform and are somewhat intricate and hazy. We have committed ourselves unreservedly to a policy of universal education, with equal opportunities to all. We have the most elaborate system for the education of our citizenship that any nation possesses and we spend more than a billion dollars annually upon it, far more than any other people. We have adopted the ambitious program of putting eight years of elementary and four years of secondary education within the reach of every child in America. We have gone far toward compelling an elementary education by law in every State in the Union. We justify our program, first, because of the necessity of preparing a citizenship that is able to participate in our democratic government, and, second, because of the desire to provide for equality of opportunity for individual development for which our democracy stands. Under older conceptions of government, monarchies, oligarchies, and aristocracies, only the leaders were educated, but in a democracy where the people are the rulers, all must have education.[2]

II. *Inspiration*

    a. Asserting a connection of the service of the teacher and the group with the maintenance of moretic values such as religious devotion, patriotism, domestic virtue, "character."

Case illustration: My heart swells within me whenever I visit Washington and stand on the marble steps and look out over our capital city, out over those great stone buildings that house the Department of State; out over the Potomac and see the white columns of Arlington. As I view that magnificent scene, my heart swells within me and thrills with pride, and I think of the power and the magnificence and the glory of my country. As I go about I see the Supreme Court dispensing righteousness. I see Congress

---

[2] Tigert, John J., "Present-Day Objectives of Education," *Add. and Proc.*, 1922, pp. 202-3.

Activities and Objectives

working upon great problems. I go down to the White House and I see the President bending over his mighty task, and I think it is a great country.

During war days I have gone out to Fort Myer, and watched the young men, the stalwart young men of our country, the rich young blood, the hope of life, marshalled there upon the field, being trained for officers for the war. I said, "They are a great group of young men, and we have a great army." I went down to the seaside and watched the great battleships as they were there in the harbor, and I said, "We have great battleships and a great navy."

Then I came home, and not many months ago on one of my visits to a country place as I came along the way, I came upon a little schoolhouse. It was one of those little, single-teacher schools that stand by the roadside in many of our States. It was standing there in the trees and looking out a little distance over a beautiful, shining lake, and the scene was attractive.

I stopped, as I always do when I pass those little institutions, and said, "I want to go in and see the teacher and see the children at their work and offer a word of greeting and encouragement." Just as I came to the schoolhouse the door opened and there stood the teacher in the doorway. Her face was lined; her hair was gray. She had given her life for the cause she loved. As she stood there, there came a little lad and she buttoned his coat about him in order to protect him from the cold, and gave him a loving look. Another boy, stalwart and strong, and she said, "I will see you tomorrow, John." Then she took a little girl in her arms and tucked her cloak about her so that she would be properly prepared for going out into the weather. As the children passed they smiled upon her and she smiled back at them.

I said, "After all, it is a magnificent country, a splendid capital, a magnificent scene at Washington, a strong government. And yet, the strength of our country rests not in our courts, not in our Congress, nor yet in our President, powerful as these sometimes are; nor in our armies or our navies. But the strength of a free government lies in the hands of the teachers who train the young and rising army for the duties and responsibilities in citizenship and in their relation to their neighbors throughout the world. . . ."[3]

    b. Increasing self-esteem of teachers by securing as speakers persons of unusual prestige, regardless of content of address. Case illustration: Address by Calvin Coolidge, *Add. and Proc.*, 1924, pp. 213-20.[4]

    c. Identifying teachers with special recognition of national heroes, as by "patriotic pilgrimages" in 1924, when the convention was held in Washington, D. C., to the Tomb of the Unknown Soldier, to the Lin-

---

[3] Thomas, Augustus O., "Education and World Progress," *Add. and Proc.*, 1923, p. 240.

[4] The report of the Resolutions Committee referred to the presence of the President as follows: "We are deeply sensible of the honor conferred upon the Nation's teachers by the President of the United States in consenting to address their representatives on the Nation's birthday. We feel that such public recognition of the dignity and importance of the profession of teaching by our Chief Magistrate at this and future conventions of the National Education Association would give inspiration and stimulus to teachers in their great endeavor." Resolutions, 1924 Convention, *Add. and Proc.*, 1924, p. 57.

coln Memorial, to Memorial Continental Hall, to the Walter Reed Memorial Hospital, to the Tomb of Woodrow Wilson, to the home of Frederick Douglass.[5]

III. *Stimulation.* Urging, by a member, or by the leader of a minority, or by an outsider with prestige, the adoption of new standards, observances, relationships, activities.

Case illustration: Due consideration should be given in all public school systems to the working out of a practical program that will permit members of different religious sects to procure for their children the desired religious instruction. But no further responsibility than the granting of time and place for this instruction must rest with the public school. No classroom teacher in the public school should attempt the work, for, just as with school nursing and school visiting, complications arise that a classroom teacher cannot cope with, and should not become involved in. The classroom teacher should never resort to dogmatic teaching or dogmatic practice of religion. She must never attempt direct religious instruction. Her part of the work should be the indirect application of such teachings and the force of example.

A program that will provide opportunity for religious instruction in the public school, according to the wishes of the parent of the child, is not impossible and can be worked out. Such a program will make not merely for the spiritual development of the individual, but will tend toward a better understanding of the motives, and a more liberal tolerance of the beliefs of others. Our united efforts in this worthy cause will clear the atmosphere of much propaganda against certain churches, and especially against the Church. As a people we have not, as yet, learned to work together harmoniously for the common good. Our individual immediate interests will be lost sight of, in the ultimate big purpose of providing in the best possible way for the spiritual welfare of the children.[6]

IV. *Educational Information.* Reporting facts and viewpoints related to the field of education, the results of investigation or experience.

Case illustration: The teaching of citizenship, like the teaching of medicine, dentistry, law, or our own profession, is fully completed only when theory is followed by practice. In the Evansville Public Schools we are trying an experiment along this line.

Throughout the year 1919-1920, there have been sent out to all the teachers of the fourth, fifth, sixth, seventh, and eighth grades so-called weekly lessons in citizenship. Number one, issued during the last week in October dealt with Halloween and the destruction of public property. The teacher was asked to read to her pupils a little story on the origin of Halloween pranks. The children were also reminded of the fact that certain playground apparatus on the public school grounds had been destroyed on Halloween with the result that it had never been replaced. The little folks had been deprived of their daily fun, coasting down the slides, etc. The

---

[5] *Add and Proc.,* 1924, pp. 221-47.

[6] Gecks, Mathilde C., "Moral and Religious Education," *Add. and Proc.,* 1924, pp. 143-44.

point was brought out that damage done to public property, like schools, has to be paid out of the money of the taxpayers, and that the term "taxpayers" really means every resident of the city whether he owns property or not, for those who pay rent simply pay their taxes indirectly. The teacher was then instructed to ask her pupils questions of this sort: What are harmless Halloween pranks? What are harmful pranks? Would it be fun to smash playground apparatus that your little brothers enjoy using? Were the school authorities right in not replacing the property which had been destroyed? Who owns the schoolhouses? Who pays for windows that are broken in them? What do you think of a boy who would smash all the windows in his own house?

The second lesson dealt with Armistice Day, the meaning of the war, and the necessity for hard work and thrift on the part of everybody in order to pay off the tremendous war debts.

A school strike which took place in a neighboring state on November 11, furnished the subject for the third lesson. The young strikers had demanded the same credit for a much shorter term and briefer hours spent in school. They had insisted on no home study and the dismissal of all teachers over twenty-five years of age. In the discussion of this incident, the children were made to see that no amount of medals or athletic prizes would help a boy if he had not earned them and was weak and anemic.[7]

V. *General Information.* Reporting facts and viewpoints not directly related to the fields of education.

Case illustration: Discussion of "The Farm Woman's Problems" by Florence E. Ward, Chief of Home Demonstration Work, U. S. Department of Agriculture (*Add. and Proc.*, 1920, pp. 75-79). The speaker presented tabulated data showing length of working day and vacation of farm women; household duties; equipment; outdoor work and keeping accounts; distances, automobiles, and telephones. Her summary and conclusions were, in part, as follows:

The five outstanding problems which the survey would indicate call for special consideration are:

1. To shorten the working day of the average farm woman
2. To lessen the amount of heavy manual labor she now performs
3. To bring about higher standards of comfort and beauty for the farm home
4. To safeguard the health of the farm family, and especially the health of the mother and the growing child
5. To develop and introduce money-yielding home industries where necessary, in order to make needed home improvements

These changes may most speedily be brought about by:

a. Introducing: (1) improved home equipment, principally running water and power machinery, and (2) more efficient methods of household management, including the rearrangement of the inconvenient kitchen and the installation of a modern heating system for the whole house.

b. Helping farm people to understand and apply the laws of nutrition and

---

[7] Benezet, L. P., "How Are We Teaching Citizenship in Our Schools?" *Add. and Proc.*, 1920, pp. 64-65.

hygiene, through home demonstrations in: (1) child care and feeding; (2) food selection for the family; (3) training in the essentials of home nursing; (4) the installation of sanitary improvements.

  c. Cultivating the idea that investment in the comfort, beauty, health, and efficiency of the farm home and community is a wise and legitimate expenditure, and perhaps the only means of stopping the drift of young people to the city.

VI. *Discussion of Affairs of Collective Group.* Proposals concerning the association's program, organization, finances, relationships; reports of committees and commissions along these lines.

Case illustration: "President's Report—Our Association and Its Work" by Jesse H. Newlon, *Add. and Proc.*, 1925, pp. 47-52. The headings of the six main divisions of the report will indicate its general character. They are as follows:

1. Work of the Association
2. The World Conference
3. Finances
4. Membership
5. Problems of Organization
6. Work of the Headquarters Staff

VII. *Discussion of Matters Affecting the Welfare of Members.* Included in this category are addresses and reports dealing with tenure, salary, retirement, homes for aged teachers, legal aid, sabbatical leave.

Case illustration: "The Teacher's Economic, Social, and Professional Welfare as Related to Tenure" by Fred M. Hunter, *Add. and Proc.*, 1927, pp. 57-65. This is in reality a report of the Committee of One Hundred on the Problems of Teachers' Tenure. It includes a discussion of the various kinds of tenure, of twelve "principles" tentatively proposed for the framing of tenure laws, of arguments for and against tenure laws, and of laws recently enacted.

VIII. *Communication of Subgroup Points of View.* Presenting, to the association as a whole, by a spokesman for a "department" or an "affiliated" organization, of points of view which may be somewhat divergent from those held by other subgroups.

Case illustration: The elementary principal is stirred by the same spirit of discovery to establish a common understanding as to his place in the world of education. He oftentimes finds himself in a position where not even tradition is present to help him plot his course. There are more than 50,000 principals of elementary schools in America, and their department is the youngest in this National Education Association. Since our organization four years ago, we have done more by working together (5,000 or 6,000 of us) than all that has been accomplished by our branch of the profession in the last forty years. We are writing books, like Mr. Watson's *Mental Measurements and the Classroom Teacher,* that are bought, and paid for, and read. We are writing magazine articles and putting out bulletins that elevate and unify, stimulate and broaden the whole profession. Our third

Yearbook, fresh from the press, is the pride of every member of the department. If one had to teach next year with just one book on Education, he might wisely choose Mr. Gist's splendid treasure house, without hesitation. Nor are we the only consumers of our co-laborers' work. The great colleges offering postgraduate work are using our first Yearbook, *The Technique of Supervision,* and the second, *The Elementary Principal in the Light of the Testing Movement,* and now *The Status and Professional Activities of the Elementary School Principal* starts forth to the honor of our entire profession; a power to uplift, to enlighten, to do much to define sharply and definitely the status of the elementary principal.

A few years ago a survey was made in the *Elementary School Journal* to classify the separate duties devolving upon the principal. A list of nearly ninety assigned responsibilities was compiled. In the four or five years since then, at least twenty more duties have been added through the introduction of dental clinics, malnutrition classes, mental testing, Schick tests, etc.

Throughout our ranks a dim uneasiness is felt. There is no unanimity of requirement on the part of school boards, nor of service on the part of the elementary principal, nor of interpretation of the principal's status by the superintendent. Our title of principal is sometimes given to the highest grade teacher of a three-room primary school, and in other places denied to the person in charge of a thousand or more pupils unless there are at least twenty-five classrooms under his care. There is still an unsettled condition where supervisors of special subjects—people expert in their line—find it hard to realize that a school must have just one head, unless confusion is to reign. It is the person responsible for coördinating all the work of all the teachers and supervisors who must be the court of decision as to how the learning process may best be served, for the schools are built and supported for the children, and for them alone. If ignorant, untrained youth could grow into good citizens without the schools, then schools need never have been built. This then is one point to be aimed at by every elementary principal in the country: to be the unquestioned head of his own school and to receive his authority from one chief, the superintendent, who represents the school board.[8]

IX. *Communication from Outside Groups.* Presentation, by a leader in some social movement or organization, of its viewpoints concerning education or child welfare or other problems.

Case illustration: A series of five addresses at the 1919 convention on the general topic, "The New World and the Demand That It Will Make Upon Public Education," the subtitles and the speakers being as follows:

  a. "Manufacturing and Commercial Interests." John H. Puelicher, Government Director of Savings, Seventh Federal Reserve District

  b. "Agricultural Interests." Henry J. Waters of the *Kansas City Star*

  c. "American Homes." Ella S. Stewart, Department of School Patrons of the National Education Association

  d. "War Education Board." Frank E. Spaulding, Head of American Education in France

[8] McSkimmon, Mary, "The Principal," *Add. and Proc.,* 1924, pp. 196-97.

e. "Organized Labor." Henry Sterling, Legislative Representative, American Federation of Labor [9]

X. *General and Educational Philosophy.* Presenting mature personal opinion as to "principles" that should actuate teachers or humanity in general; preachments.

Case illustration: I can best begin by pointing out a defect in the ideal of democracy as I have thus far presented it, namely, the lack of completeness, of final or substantive character, in either the political or the social definition of democracy. There is an aesthetic or perhaps a moral fault in both, for dearly won and precious as they are, nevertheless they stand as means and not as ends. They clear the way for democracy, establish it as a form, but do not tell it what to do. Will man be content that there shall be no interference among them with each other's dues, no privilege or tyranny? Political democracy lies too close to the mere conception of individual rights to be a final social philosophy. It is not enough that men should stop trespassing upon each other's fields. If religion, especially Christianity, does not mock us, men have a work to do together, a work which transcends the personal fortunes of any single man, or all these taken in their aggregate as separate interests. Nor is it enough that every man shall have his chance. His chance for what? Have life and liberty no end but the pursuit of happiness? The canker of separateness and isolation lies at the heart of every individualistic theory of human good. It is not enough that the road should be open to talent. It is not even enough that each shall make the most of himself for the common good. The common good must be known and consciously advanced: there must be participation in it and in the achievement of it. Political democracy emphasizes the distinction between men as equals: to each his own, equality before the law. Philanthropic democracy calls for human sympathy and kindness: *noblesse oblige.* Each leaves us with a view of men struggling separately, individually, either to maintain and advance their own purposes, although with fairness and even with kindness and helpfulness, or sacrificing themselves as individuals to other individuals. Neither presents a picture of men working together for universal ends. Completed democracy pictures a community of interests, not a uniform life but a unity of purpose, an understanding shared by all, a fate which all help to advance, a mastery of nature and its own character on the part of humanity in common. The ideal of democracy finds its fulfillment, I submit, in the conception of mankind united in knowledge, in faith, in purpose, in action, and in command over the forces of life. [10]

XI. *Formal Expressions.* Addresses of welcome by the mayor of the convention city and by other dignitaries, responses by officers of the association or by appointed members, presentation of gavel, formal greetings from other groups, memorial addresses in honor of deceased educational leaders.

These are so easily recognized by the casual reader of the convention proceedings that it is not necessary to cite an illustration.

---

[9] *Add. and Proc.,* 1919, pp. 47-64.

[10] Holmes, Henry W., "The Responsibility of the College and the University in a Democracy," *Add. and Proc.,* 1922, p. 247.

It is recognized that a classification of units of communication that are as large as these papers and addresses cannot be made with any claim to complete objectivity or accuracy. If each of the prepared papers were broken up into several parts, perhaps in some cases as many parts as there are paragraphs, greater analytical accuracy might be achieved. It would no doubt be discovered that one or more paragraphs of a long discussion which is classed as "interpretation" should be called "information," and that a few should be included under the heading of "inspiration." However, it is submitted that this process of fracturing a unit of discussion into paragraphs would produce a less valid understanding of the objectives and the results of this form of communication than would the use of the large unit without fracturing. No paragraph can be understood apart from its setting. Many paragraphs are merely incidental; others, sometimes a very few or even a single one in a long address, will be of significance in determining how the address should be classified.

It should be noted that these addresses are given to the general membership, not to the Representative Assembly nor to any other group of chosen leaders although some of the leaders would usually be present. The number of listeners varies from one or two thousand to eight or ten thousand. In some instances, considerable numbers of persons who are not teachers pay membership fees in order to be permitted to hear an address by some well-known speaker, although it is probably always true that a great majority of the listeners are teachers. The matters discussed receive no formal action on the part of the audience. The only immediate measure of approval of the points of view presented is the applause, and this is not recorded. Other measures would be found in action taken later by various groups of leaders, such for example as the adoption of a resolution by the Representative Assembly or the creation of a committee. The meetings, especially those that are addressed by persons of wide public recognition, are likely to be reported somewhat extensively in the newspapers.

Before the addresses, it is customary to have a prayer by a local clergyman and to have, also, one or more musical numbers.

These addresses are to be interpreted thus:

1. As furnishing a means of direct, face-to-face communication of information and attitudes from the leaders of the association to the membership, supplementing the printed communication in *The*

Journal and in letters and bulletins. Not all the members are present, it is true, nor a very large percentage of them, but those that are in attendance can be effectively reached. Through these, and through the newspaper reports of the sessions, many others receive at least some of the points of view presented. The speakers are not usually the official leaders of the group, but since they are chosen by the official leaders, it may be assumed that their statements are not in serious conflict with the views of the leaders in controversial matters. The response of the crowd, through applause, is not necessarily an accurate representation of the reasoned opinion of the members, however, because of the relation of mass to suggestibility.[11] The enthusiasm of the crowd with regard to any proposal made can certainly not be accepted as of any significance in determining the need for making appropriations of money for carrying out a speaker's suggestions, or the need for appointing a committee to deal with the matter, or even the propriety of adopting a resolution.

2. They are to be interpreted as a means of indirect communication of association points of view to the general public. The general sessions are of considerable news interest because of their size and because of the fact that educational leaders of the greatest prestige, as well as others of wide recognition, are commonly found on their programs. That the newspapers report with some accuracy what the speakers have said is made comparatively certain by the maintenance of a convention press service by a division of the headquarters staff.[12]

3. Those addresses classified as interpretation, stimulation, educational and general information, and educational and general philosophy would be appropriately presented to relatively juvenile, untrained teachers by relatively mature, well-trained teachers as a means of orienting the former in the traditional and current aspects of the occupation of teaching. It is impossible to determine the experience or the training of the persons in attendance, but in view of the fact that the membership is drawn most largely from village

[11] Cf. Allport, F. H., *Social Psychology*, p. 249: "A situation which speedily places one in an attitude of submissive suggestibility is the presence of a group, or indeed the mere allusion to large numbers. We bow before the will of the majority. We rise irresistibly when the congregation rises, clap when the audience claps, and express disapproval in unison with the throng. . . ."
Bogardus, E. S., *Fundamentals of Social Psychology*, p. 255, declares: "The force of numbers overwhelms the individual."
See also Sidis, B., *The Psychology of Suggestion*, pp. 299-300.
[12] Pp. 104-5 of the present study.

and city school systems, a considerable and an increasing amount of training may be assumed. This would point to a decreasing propriety in presenting these kinds of communications. However, because educational ideas and standards and practices are constantly changing, addresses of the categories just mentioned may be highly proper as a means of reorientation, or orientation in new phases of education, even though it be assumed that all listeners have had much training and much experience in the educational field.

4. Discussions of the affairs of the collective group and of the welfare of members are practical matters, requiring action by one or more of the leadership bodies. Their inclusion in the general sessions is apparently for the purpose of securing wider interest and support for projects which these leadership subgroups are considering, or for the purpose of crystallizing the views of the leaders as to steps to be taken, through observation of the responses of the larger number present at the general sessions. This might be interpreted, therefore, as an attempted sharing of responsibility on the part of the leaders.

5. The communication of subgroup points of view is manifestly for the purpose of unifying the membership, and perhaps indirectly the whole teaching population, through promoting better understanding of the special activities and problems of the more or less specialized subgroups. It involves a tacit recognition of potential conflict across occupational subgroup lines. Sessions at which these topics are discussed may be considered in reality joint sessions of the departments.

6. Communications from outside groups are objective examples of the play of diverse influences upon education and upon an educational organization.[13] Quite obviously, only the representatives of those groups whose aims and purposes are not in serious conflict with those of the association are invited to appear on the programs. The platform does not constitute an open forum, but a carefully controlled channel of communication.

7. The situation is probably one in which there will be the most widespread, spontaneous approval of addresses classified as inspiration. The massing of large numbers of persons, all of them group-conscious for the time being, and having much in common in their religious and patriotic and moral and occupational standards, and being conscious of what they have in common, is itself a phenome-

---

[13] Cf. Counts, G. S., *School and Society in Chicago.*

non that is "inspiring." [14] Suggestions in harmony with those that lie in the situation itself will be spontaneously approved.

8. Detailed reports of objective experimentation and observation are almost completely lacking in all the categories. The situation is not a proper one for the submission and evaluation of data. Such reports are, in their very nature, more or less out of harmony with the "inspiring" character of the situation in that they involve reason rather than feeling.[15]

9. The general sessions obviously furnish opportunity for a considerable number of persons engaged in education and related fields of work to secure public recognition. Speakers on these programs are, for the time being at least, national figures, and such recognition is no doubt highly prized by many. Because it is interpreted in somewhat vicarious fashion, it is likely to be more or less prized also by the professional groups to which these individuals belong, by the geographic regions and political divisions from which they come, and perhaps in the case of women, by others of their own sex.

10. Even though it is recognized, as indicated in the foregoing paragraphs, that there are certain values in these general sessions, the question may well be raised as to whether these meetings are worth what they cost. The total money cost of convention attendance on the part of 8,000 to 10,000 persons is obviously a large sum. The cost to the association, not only in money, but in the time and energy of its officers, is likewise very great. These meetings of the general membership have lost some of the significance which they had under the town-meeting system of association government, for part of them were then policy-making, business sessions. They have lost some of the significance which they had in an earlier period when teachers were less well trained than they are at present and when relatively more of their training was secured through gatherings like these, ranging from local "institutes" to national conventions. Not only are teachers better trained than formerly, through courses of increased duration in normal schools, teachers colleges, and schools of education, but printed professional material in the form of books and periodicals is available in greater amounts. Moreover, through such technological devices as the radio, direct communication is being established between educational leaders on the one hand and the teaching population and general population on

[14] Allport, F. H., *op. cit.*, p. 316. Bogardus, E. S., *op. cit.*, p. 255.
[15] Bogardus, E. S., *op. cit.*, pp. 254-55.

Activities and Objectives

the other hand.[16] The question of the advisability of discontinuing the general sessions cannot be answered within the scope of the present study, but in view of the changed and changing conditions just mentioned the association might well give careful consideration to the matter.[17]

Convention Resolutions. Another characteristic set of activities in connection with the annual convention is the discussion and adoption of formal resolutions, prepared during the preceding year by a committee composed of one delegate from each state.[18] Until the amendment of the by-laws in 1928, the work of the committee was done while the convention was in session, but from now on it may be assumed that most of the resolutions will be formulated in advance of the meeting. What effect this new rule will have on the nature of the reports remains to be seen.

The committee makes its report to the Representative Assembly, which may amend and supplement the report. This is a recurring, characteristic activity on the part of the group. It has set up this machinery with the obvious intention of communicating its points of view "to whom it may concern," and it uses the machinery. It is therefore important to record and to analyze pronouncements of the resolutions committee.

In Table IX is to be found a complete tabulation of the matters covered by the resolutions adopted during the period under discussion. These are classified under seven headings, as shown in the table itself.

Perhaps the most impressive fact brought out by the tabulation is that of variety. In eleven years the association has declared itself on no less than 123 different matters, general and specific. Seventy-

---

[16] Pp. 102-3 of the present study.

[17] Of course the propriety of annual meetings of the Representative Assembly and other official bodies is not here questioned.

[18] By-laws, Article VI, Section 2: On the first day of the annual meeting of the Association, at such time and place as shall be designated on the annual program by the President of the Association, the accredited delegates to the Representative Assembly from each state shall elect one member and one alternate who are active members of the Association for each of the following committees, to serve for the ensuing year: Credentials, Resolutions, and Necrology. . . .

Sec. 3. The Committee on Resolutions shall report at the annual business meeting of the Representative Assembly, and except by unanimous consent, all resolutions shall be referred to said committee without discussion. This committee shall receive and consider all resolutions proposed by active members, or referred to it by the president; some time during the second day of the annual meeting of the Association the committee shall hold a meeting, at a place and time to be announced in the printed program, for the purpose of receiving proposed resolutions and hearing those who may wish to advocate them. *Add. and Proc.*, 1928, p. 1028.

TABLE IX

A Complete Tabulation by Years and a Classification of Resolutions Adopted by the National Education Association at Its Annual Conventions, 1918 to 1928

Resolution	1918	1919	1920	1921	1922	1923	1924	1925	1926	1927	1928
1. General Professional Matters											
Favoring adequate program of physical education....	x	x	x	x		x	x	x		x	x
Favoring citizenship training including patriotism and the Constitution of United States	x	x	x	x	x		x	x			
Favoring extension of the health program...........	x		x			x		x		x	x
Urging measures equalizing educational opportunity..	x		x			x	x	x	x		
Favoring school publicity.......................	x							x			
Approving English language as a vehicle of instruction.	x	x	x	x							
Favoring national university.....................	x										
Declaring responsibility of nation to share educational costs...	x										
Favoring socialized schools.......................	x										
Urging civic and social training for girls.............	x										
Opposing dual system of schools..................	x										
Favoring national department of education..........		x	x	x	x	x	x	x	x	x	x
Favoring improvement of rural education...........		x	x	x	x	x					
Favoring adult and continuation classes............		x	x							x	
Favoring increased state-wide financing of education...		x		x	x	x				x	x
Urging adequate financial support of public schools....		x					x	x	x		
Urging enlargement of local district school unit........		x		x		x		x		x	
Favoring vocational education....................		x	x								
Favoring special classes for disadvantaged..........		x							x		
Urging plans for recruiting teachers...............		x									
Urging better state laws dealing with education......		x									
Urging effective compulsory attendance laws........		x									
Favoring compulsory thrift instruction.............		x									
Favoring international coöperation and organization of teachers....................................		x									
Favoring a bureau of international study...........		x									
Advocating a year of compulsory civic, physical, and vocational training at public expense.............		x									
Justifying large expenditures for education..........\			x	x		x					
Urging housing of schools adequate for full sessions....			x								
Declaring vocational education must not overshadow cultural.......................................			x								
Declaring against federal domination in vocational education......................................			x								
Favoring highest recognition of state superintendents..			x								
Favoring teaching of social hygiene in teacher-training institutions...............................			x								
Favoring promotion of international educational relations...			x								
Favoring state supervision of public and private schools..			x								
Favoring selection of highest type of citizen for school board..			x								

Activities and Objectives

TABLE IX (Continued)

Resolution	1918	1919	1920	1921	1922	1923	1924	1925	1926	1927	1928
1. General Professional Matters (Continued)											
Declaring for choice of administrative officers by elected boards			x								
Favoring longer school year			x								
Favoring compulsory education through high school period			x								
Declaring education a state responsibility				x	x						
Urging use of war revenues for education				x							
Opposing financial domination of school boards by municipal authorities				x	x						
Urging teaching respect and obedience for law				x				x	x		
Urging federal aid for territories as well as states				x	x						
Favoring truthful history, international as well as national				x							
Favoring professional non-political leadership				x							
Endorsing World Conference on Education and World Federation of Education Associations				x				x	x		x
Approving anti-narcotic education					x				x		
Favoring observance of American Education Week					x						
Urging program of character education					x						
Favoring teaching the history of public education					x						
Urging economical spending of school money						x					
Opposing admission of outside agencies to schools						x	x				
Supporting program of organized and controlled athletic sports							x				
Urging greater recognition of scholarship							x				
Urging clearing of titles of school lands							x				
Favoring individualization of curriculum								x			
Favoring legal specification of school board's and superintendent's authority								x			
Declaring pupil's failure and repetition abnormal								x			
Declaring educational and vocational guidance a school obligation								x			
Favoring non-partisan school boards (elected)								x			
Favoring long overlapping terms for board members								x			
Opposing legislative interference with curriculum								x			
Favoring giving more functions to State Department								x			
Supporting exclusive right of superintendent to nominate teachers and employees								x			
Supporting exclusive right of superintendent and supervisors to propose curricula, textbooks, educational supplies								x			
Favoring requiring superintendent to submit annual unit cost budget report										x	
Favoring laying out building program as prerogative of superintendent										x	
Favoring requirement that superintendent's reports be based on scientific inquiry										x	
Favoring special federal aid for education in flood areas										x	
Commending national Congress of Parents and Teachers and promising coöperation											x

TABLE IX (Continued)

Resolution	1918	1919	1920	1921	1922	1923	1924	1925	1926	1927	1928
1. General Professional Matters (Continued)											
Favoring investigation of additional source of school revenue											x
Approving study of curriculum											x
Favoring courses of study in international relations											x
Favoring unified education administration with business superintendent subordinate to superintendent of education											x
Asking greater financial support for Federal Bureau of Education											x
2. Professional Standards											
Urging adequate teacher-training facilities		x	x	x	x	x	x				
Favoring adequate professional training of teachers		x	x	x	x	x	x	x	x	x	
Urging teachers to join local, state, and National Education Association		x		x				x			
Supporting four years' training beyond high school for teachers			x							x	
Favoring promotion on merit							x	x			
Supporting teacher's rights to professional initiative and academic freedom							x				x
Urging creation of code of professional ethics								x			
Imposing on teachers the obligation to participate in civic activities								x			
Favoring raising teachers to professional status									x		
Urging special training for administrators and supervisors										x	
Asking summer schools to avoid conflict with National Education Association convention days											x
3. Welfare of Teachers											
Favoring adequate salaries for teachers	x	x	x	x	x	x	x			x	
Supporting the single salary schedule			x	x	x						
Favoring retirement allowances for teachers			x	x	x	x	x	x	x	x	x
Favoring tenure laws			x	x	x	x	x	x	x	x	x
Opposing salary discrimination on basis of sex							x				
Favoring minimum salary for teachers								x			
Favoring sabbatical leave for teachers									x		
4. Support for Members in Specific Conflicts											
Favoring improved schools in city of Washington					x	x	x				
Disapproving removal of Pennsylvania State Commissioner							x				
Opposing income tax for federal-employed teachers							x	x			
Protesting removal of New York City superintendent							x				
5. Social Problems Related to Field of Education											
Favoring Americanization of foreign-born	x	x	x	x		x	x				x
Urging eradication of illiteracy	x	x	x	x	x	x	x		x	x	x
Opposing child labor, favoring federal amendment	x					x	x	x	x		
Approving college military units	x										

Activities and Objectives

TABLE IX (Continued)

RESOLUTION	1918	1919	1920	1921	1922	1923	1924	1925	1926	1927	1928
5. *Social Problems Related to Field of Education* (Cont.)											
Commending Junior Red Cross..................	x										
Favoring compulsory registration of minors.........		x									
Opposing cigarette smoking.....................			x								
Supporting literacy tests for citizenship............								x	x		
Endorsing program of National Conference on Outdoor Recreation.............................								x			
Opposing circulation of obscene matter............									x	x	
Favoring reduction of postage on books............										x	x
6. *General Social Problems, Not Directly Related to Education*											
Favoring woman suffrage amendment.............	x	x	x								
Approving Eighteenth Amendment................	x	x									
Approving League of Nations....................			x								
Favoring law enforcement......................							x				
Urging measures for world peace.................							x	x	x	x	x
7. *Miscellaneous Declarations*											
Expressing confidence in the president of the United States..	x										
Favoring conscription for selective service during war	x										
Expressing appreciation for patriotic spirit of Congress	x										
Miscellaneous war resolutions...................	x										
Insisting on budget system for public appropriations...	x										
Supporting coöperation with American Legion.......			x								
Pledging loyalty to American institutions and ideals...			x								
Welcoming coöperation of American Bar Association...							x				
Endorsing George Rogers Clark Memorial..........										x	
Congratulating Mrs. Evangeline Lindbergh on the achievements of her son.......................											x

seven of the statements (63 per cent) have been made only once, while on six matters the association has reaffirmed its position at nine of the eleven conventions, and on three issues at ten conventions. The remaining declarations have been repeated from two to eight times, consecutively or intermittently.

The number of times that a particular matter is mentioned in these formal pronouncements is not an accurate measure of universality of interest nor of depth of conviction in regard to it. In fact, its complete omission might be considered objective proof that there is no doubt in anyone's mind as to the prevalent opinion upon it. This fact is well illustrated in an incident occurring at the 1927 convention. When a delegate complained that the committee had omitted a resolution supporting world peace, he was informed that there was no need of it. "I think it is almost like readopting the Ten Commandments," said the president of the association. "We are all in favor of it."[19]

The mere act of formulating and publishing a first or a later statement of position on an issue involves the implication that there is doubt as to what the position of the group is and the further implication that it wishes to remove that doubt. This may not be the case, however. The factor of timeliness or opportunism may be the determining one, as it was in the instance just cited, when the delegates' demand for support of world peace was based on the fact that a world-peace conference was in session. A current, definite statement has a news value, a value in communication with other groups and with the general public, which an old declaration or an assumed, unformulated statement of group attitude does not have. This fact accounts for repetitions.

Sometimes a formal statement is followed by the creation of a committee, which engages in activity designed to carry out the intent of the resolution. So long as the committee continues active, the association is likely to renew its declaration from year to year. This is illustrated in such cases as that of the Legislative Commission, whose primary function has been that of attempting to secure the creation of a national Department of Education, and of the committees on tenure and retirement allowances. While the record of adopted resolutions is not by itself significant as to the policies and real activities of the association, this record when taken in connection with that of the creation and continuance and instruction of committees and executive divisions is significant.

Of course the group does not adopt a resolution until it receives a suggestion from some source inside or outside its ranks. It then must act, favorably or unfavorably. The fact that it has responded favorably so many times to a suggestion that it support new proposals is evidence of the tacit assumption that the action will conciliate minorities within the membership who seek support for their special projects, and will promote good feeling on the part of outside groups that ask coöperation in their enterprises. It is a procedure of internal and external accommodation. So long as the group believes that it has little at stake it is to be expected that it will lend its name and prestige to almost any proposal not in direct opposition to its special interests, just as individual members of a group gladly surrender to their leaders' authority in matters that are considered

[19] *Add. and Proc.*, 1927, p. 1097.

Activities and Objectives

minor.[20] But there is more at stake than may be discerned on the surface.

The adoption of such a great variety of resolutions creates the impression of scattered energy. It must be admitted that not so great an amount of energy is involved as might be assumed, however, for the act of adopting the resolution appears to be the only action taken concerning most of the matters dealt with in these formal statements. The best and the worst that can be said about these declarations that are not followed up by the creation of a machinery for making them effective is what Alexander said in 1910 about the resolutions designed to influence national legislation—that they are "rather futile." [21]

The multiplicity of resolutions also produces the impression of lack of definite policy and objective. As one writer has expressed it, in commenting on teachers' organizations in general: [22]

> These existing organizations rarely formulate or consistently pursue definite social policies. They frequently express lofty ideals in resolutions and then proceed to neglect their offspring as the codfish neglects its eggs. Their aspirations are but seed sown on the rock or else fleecy summer clouds that are speedily dissolved in thin air. Not so do strong social groups cherish their ideals and their policies.

There is reason to believe that the resolutions, even at the particular time when they are adopted, are not always an accurate reflection of the opinion of a majority of the association members, because:

1. The adoption by the Representative Assembly of the report of the Committee on Resolutions may come as the result of passive assent to the declarations formulated rather than as a result of active thinking on the part of the delegates.[23]
2. It may likewise be true that a few leaders within the committee are the only active participants in formulating the statements.[24]
3. Some of the leaders in formulating these statements probably consider their proper function that of declaring what the members ought to believe and support rather than that of reflecting what their position actually is.

---

[20] Ross, E. A., *Principles of Sociology*, p. 275.
[21] Appendix, pp. 173-76 of the present study.
[22] Snedden, David, "The Professional Improvement of Teachers and Teaching Through Organization," *School and Society*, X (Nov. 8, 1919), pp. 531-39.
[23] See Supplement, pp. 167-72 of the present study.
[24] See Supplement, pp. 167-72 of the present study.

In other words, although the resolutions are made to appear to be formal communications from the association as a whole to other social groups, in reality all that can be said with assurance about them is that they are communications from a few, sometimes a very few, persons who chance to be in a position to formulate them. So far as they fail to reflect the opinions of the membership, they might properly be classified as a means of control exercised by the pro tempore leaders upon the membership.

Even though it is true that the adoption of a resolution is in many instances the only action taken by the association upon a particular issue, there being no appointment of a subgroup for working along the lines indicated in the declaration, and no appropriation of funds, still it must be evident that the mere fact of calling attention to a new need or a new issue naturally tends to divert group attention from other matters. Setting up a large number of foci of attention would certainly result in a relatively weak concentration of group attention upon any one focus, weak either because on the average only a small fraction of the membership concentrates its attention upon it, or because the group as a whole can devote only a small fraction of its attention to it. If the adoption of resolutions were commonly followed by subsidization of committees for carrying out the intent of the resolutions, the creation of a great number of such subgroups would result in the inadequate support of many or possibly of all of them from the limited funds of the organization. In other words, wide scattering of the energy and the resources of the association is a possibility under the present scheme of formulation of official statements of policy.

Moreover, there is the possibility of division within the membership, due to the fact that resolutions in which only a small minority have an active interest may be adopted by the Representative Assembly. As pointed out elsewhere in this study, more than five-sixths of the delegates each year are "new" and, in what is essentially a large-crowd situation, likely to give passive assent to whatever propositions may be recommended by those who happen to be in positions of leadership. Opposing minorities, persons of potential leadership who are not at that time in a position to formulate their own particular points of view and to present them for the assent of the crowd, aware of the superficiality of the crowd action and the lack of meaning even in unanimous action under such circumstances, but aware, too, of the futility of opposition, are likely to "refuse to have anything more to do with the association"—to withdraw from the organization or to become inactive in it.[25]

With the chance or intentional appointment to service on the Resolutions Committee of persons differing in points of view from some of their predecessors comes the possibility of an official statement not consistent with preceding statements, a product of the active interest of a new minority and of the passive assent of a new Representative Assembly. It is of course not proposed that the association should not change its position on issues. It should do so officially whenever the views of its members actually change, but not until then. The present method of adopting official points of view magnifies the possibility of the appearance of over-frequent change—a possibility which carries with it the prospect of loss of professional and public confidence in the association.

All these undesirable possibilities—scattering of energy and resources, division within the membership, inconsistency—could be largely obviated (1) if the issues officially recognized by the organization were limited to the number which it can support with an adequate committee personnel and adequate financial appropriations; and (2) if the principles were declared only after securing an expression from the professional members, as distinct from the "casual, juvenile members." [26] This expression should be secured, not at conventions, because they are not representative and because they meet under conditions that are not conducive to deliberation, but by a survey or consensus procedure. "Professional members" might be defined as all members of a certain number of years' standing or might be defined on any other basis that would insure the representation of all occupational subgroups at the same time that it provides the certainty of mature, responsible, professional judgment. If it is agreed by the leadership that available funds will permit the active support of five issues, let the professional membership determine by a preferential voting scheme which five are most urgent. Then let these be supported vigorously for a long enough period to produce the result desired or until a shifting of conditions renders other issues more urgent, as determined by a consensus of the group.[27]

[25] The writer has discovered a few instances of this outcome. It would be manifestly unethical to report the names of the individuals concerned.
[26] Snedden, David, *op. cit.*, pp. 531-32.
[27] A consensus procedure such as is here proposed is used by the United States Chamber of Commerce.

CHAPTER VI

ACTIVITIES AND OBJECTIVES *(Continued)*

ACTIVITIES OF THE EXECUTIVE STAFF

An organization as large as this one necessarily employs a staff of specialists to keep records and accounts and to attend to a certain amount of intra-group communication. These functions are an irreducible minimum, determined by the fact of organization. Beyond this minimum, other functions may be undertaken, their kind and extent being determined by such factors as special group interest, economic resources, personnel of leadership, personnel of membership.

The executive staff of the National Education Association, as pointed out in an earlier chapter, is organized in eight divisions: Accounts, Field and Legislative Service, Business, Publications, Research, Classroom Service, Administrative Service (Department of Superintendence), Records and Membership. The functions of the Division of Accounts, the Division of Business, and of the records section of the Division of Records and Membership are evident from their names. The membership section of the last-named division has already been discussed.[1] The activities of the remaining divisions will now be described.

Legislative Division. A special division is maintained with the avowed aim of securing the enactment of certain laws, especially one creating a Federal Department of Education, with a secretary in the president's cabinet. This is one of the issues upon which the association has not changed its position in ten years. Its annual resolutions have affirmed and reaffirmed the demand for this form of federal recognition of education. The position of field secretary was created in 1918, one of the principal obligations of the office being to promote public interest in this measure. For two years, 1922 to 1924, the Division of Field Work was in reality two divisions, called Field Work and Legislative Work, respectively, each with a direc-

---

[1] Chap. II of the present study.

Activities and Objectives

tor. Since 1924, it has been called the Division of Legislative Service, or simply the Legislative Division. It is in the charge of a legislative secretary with assistants and clerical aids. Its work is carried on in coöperation with the Legislative Commission of the association, this commission having a membership at present of 129 from all the states.

The kinds of activities have been, from the beginning, as follows:

1. Addresses in favor of the Education Bill, by the secretary of the Legislative Division, at large educational and other public meetings; also addresses by other leaders in the association, arranged for by the Legislative Division.
2. Direct appeal to congressmen during interviews, by the legislative secretary and others.
3. Distribution of printed pamphlets, explaining and supporting the measure, to persons and organizations.
4. Arranging public hearings on the bill during sessions of Congress.
5. Organizing the membership to exert pressure on congressmen.
6. Securing the coöperation of other groups in bringing pressure to bear on congressmen, by means of formal resolutions and communications favoring the bill, and by attendance at public hearings.
7. Securing general publicity by the use of newspaper and magazine material, debate material, and the radio.
8. Distributing literature favoring the bill at Republican and Democratic national conventions (1928) and attempting, through the activities of party delegates favorable to the bill, to secure its endorsement in the party platforms.
9. Reporting the division's activities and their apparent results to the membership.

The 1928 report of the Legislative Division gives the following summaries: [2]

> The field secretary spent 171 days in the field, traveling 30,900 miles, and visited 18 states and 32 cities, making return visits to a number of these. In all, 45 addresses were made on the Education Bill, while conferences for furthering the cause were numerous. Several new folders on the Education Bill were published, and these, along with other literature on the subject, were given widespread distribution to study groups and debaters in every

[2] *Annual Report of the Secretary,* National Education Association, Minneapolis, July, 1928, pp. 43-44.

state of the Union, the District of Columbia, and Hawaii. Altogether 205,840 pamphlets, including the bill itself, were sent out. Letters written in answer to inquiries about the bill and in promotion of organization work in the states numbered 4,327, in addition to 42,328 multigraphed form letters.

During the year the number of supporting organizations for a Department of Education has been raised to 31. Reindorsement of the movement has been made in unmistakable terms by a number of these associations within recent months.

At the present time every state in the Union has a chairman appointed to direct the activities in behalf of a Department of Education with the exception of four—Maryland, New Jersey, New Hampshire, and Idaho. A congressional district chairman has been appointed for the same purpose in each congressional district in 35 states.

The attempt to lead the members themselves into active participation in the effort to secure the establishment of a Department of Education is well illustrated in the legislative commission's report at the 1926 convention: [3]

> It is our job to see that our representatives are informed. They must be made to understand why the profession is supporting the Curtis-Reed Bill. Nothing less than a personal discussion of the matter with Senators and Representatives can be counted upon to do the job. We must go over its provisions with them, section by section. . . .
>
> In order to accomplish the results . . . it will be necessary to have the full coöperation of state and local educational associations throughout the nation. It is only as you teachers, principals and superintendents of schools, thoroughly believing in the importance of our cause, present it for the consideration of laymen and in coöperation with them bring the matter to the attention of our representatives, that the campaign can be won.

The general policy seems to be to print only the arguments favorable to the proposal. For example, in *The Journal* for May, 1927 (p. 161) after attention was called to the availability of material covering the question, "Should there be a national department of education?" the affirmative arguments were printed in full, while the negative ones were completely lacking.

This division is a specialized agency established and maintained primarily for the achievement of one of the specific objectives of the association, namely, the establishment of a Federal Department of Education, and concerning itself only incidentally with other legislative matters. It engages in intra-group communication and leadership and organization, all within the limits set by its special objective. It engages in extra-group communication and propaganda;

[3] *Add. and Proc.*, 1926, p. 222.

it enters into open conflict with some of the groups opposed to the achievement of its goal; it seeks the active coöperation of influential organizations in its efforts to accomplish its single purpose. There is as yet no objective evidence, in the form of favorable action by responsible bodies such as congressional committees, as to the effectiveness of its various activities.

There are two factors which undoubtedly have developed cumulatively to lessen the chances of success of the campaign for a Federal Department of Education. One is the organized opposition coming from such groups as the Catholic Church and the United States Chamber of Commerce. Opposition has had time to develop and to organize.

The other is the lessening of the nationalistic tendency in the attack on problems, the tendency to seek through national organization a solution of all problems that appeared to have significance in relation to national security and well-being. Sentiment in favor of this procedure apparently reached its peak during the war at about the time of the creation of the Commission on the Emergency in Education and has apparently declined quite rapidly during the latter part of the period of this study. The association, evidently in recognition of these two factors, has modified its position somewhat, being willing to support the establishment of a federal department with functions fewer and subsidies much less than those contemplated in the bills introduced by friendly congressmen early in the period of this study. There is at least some basis for the belief that if the association had asked for the enactment of its present proposal earlier, before the natural opponents of such a measure had time to organize their opposition, and while a strong national spirit was widely prevalent, it might have achieved success.

From a consideration of social and industrial and political developments in the United States it seems certain that education will become more nationalized than it is at present. This will come about as a natural adjustment to changing conditions, conditions such as nation-wide integration in industry, increasing ineffectiveness of local and state taxing systems in their relation to nation-wide business groups, increasing mobility of population due to improved communication and transportation, and, probably, a tendency toward industrial representation in government as contrasted with representation on a geographic basis. Agitation on the part of this association for increasing participation by the national government in the organization and support of education may hasten the changes which would normally come slowly. It may speed them up sufficiently that the customary institutional "lag" will be reduced to a minimum.[4] This would be, of course, highly desirable from the standpoint of the social engineer. To spend great effort, however, in an attempt to establish a new social mechanism in advance of a social, economic, and industrial situation which demands it, is futile. The association may do well to inquire very carefully into all factors in the situation before continuing to devote its Legislative Division's efforts and funds exclusively to one end.

Division of Publications. 1. *The Bulletin.* For several years prior to the period with which this study deals, the association had maintained a printed "bulletin" as a means of communication with its members. Volume I, No. 1, appeared in April, 1913. It contained twelve pages, was of the same size as the ordinary railway folder, and had the same double-column arrangement. Announcement was made that it would be issued quarterly.

> The September number will contain information for the benefit of those members who were not present at the summer meeting—such as the list of officers elected, the resolutions adopted, and a short summary of the proceedings of the meeting. The December number will contain the program and announcements for the meeting of the Department of Superintendence. The March number will contain a summary of the business transacted at the superintendents' meeting, and a general outline of the plans for the summer meeting. The June number will contain the program and detailed arrangements for the summer meeting.

In addition to the foregoing announcement concerning *The Bulletin* itself, this first number gave brief items of information about the convention to be held at Salt Lake City the following July: reduced

---

[4] ... The various parts of modern culture are not changing at the same rate, some parts are changing much more rapidly than others; and since there is a correlation and interdependence of parts a rapid change in one part of our culture requires readjustment through other changes in the various correlated parts of culture. For instance, industry and education are correlated, hence a change in industry makes adjustments necessary through changes in the educational system. Industry and education are two variables, and if the change in industry occurs and the adjustment through education follows, industry may be referred to as the independent variable and education as the dependent variable. Where one part of culture changes first, through some discovery or invention, and occasions changes in some part of culture dependent upon it, there frequently is a delay in the changes occasioned in the dependent part of culture. The extent of this lag will vary according to the nature of the cultural material, but may exist for a considerable number of years, during which time there may be said to be a maladjustment. It is desirable to reduce the period of maladjustment, to make the cultural adjustments as quickly as possible.—Ogburn, W. F., *Social Change*, pp. 200-1.

Activities and Objectives 99

railroad rates; personnel of committee on arrangements and on "securing a large attendance at Salt Lake City"; hotels, names of persons responsible for the program; list of organizations which would meet at the same time as the association. There was also a brief account of the meeting of the Department of Superintendence the preceding February, including names of officers chosen and a report of the resolutions adopted. Explanation was made of a plan to raise "A Million Dollar Fund for the National Education Association, . . . for expert studies and the distribution of results to educators of all grades. . . . It is expected," the statement continued, "that Educators and Benevolent Wealth will answer this call for advancing the great cause of American Education."

Succeeding issues were constructed on much the same pattern as the first number, containing from sixteen to thirty-two pages. However, the February, 1914 number was entitled *Yearbook and List of Active Members* and contained, besides the roster of names, certain formal records, such as the Act of Incorporation and By-Laws, names of officers and minutes of meetings. This number comprised 386 pages. The custom of printing the February number as a yearbook continued for several years, and another number, published in May, included the proceedings of the Department of Superintendence. *The Bulletin* of 1917-1918 ranged in size from twenty-four to forty-eight pages, with a yearbook of 404 pages as the February number, and was issued six times during the year. It was no longer a mere bulletin of more or less formal announcements, but it included brief abstracts of addresses and editorials dealing with a variety of matters of interest to teachers. Beginning in September, 1919, *The Bulletin* was issued monthly.

2. *The Journal.* *The Journal of the National Education Association* replaced *The Bulletin* in January, 1921, and an editor was employed; he headed the editorial department, later called the Division of Publications. *The Journal* contained twenty pages, quarto size, at the start, with "32 or even 48 pages" recommended in the first annual report of the editorial department.[5] It was also proposed (1) that the material should be more varied, more space should be given to the interests of the departments of the association; (2) that special emphasis should be devoted to the work of the state and local associations; (3) that more space should be devoted to the plans and purposes of the association, and to work actually accomplished

[5] *Add. and Proc.,* 1921, p. 236.

or under way; and (4) that there should be a section devoted to advance in the science of education. Prompted by expressed or anticipated misgivings on the part of educational periodicals, *The Journal* disclaimed any attempt "to take the place of other educational magazines." The secretary of the association reiterated the same statement in his own report when he said: [6]

> We should keep in mind the fact that *The Journal* is established for the single purpose of promoting the interests of the association. It should ever remain the mouthpiece of the association and should never allow itself to aspire to control the whole field of educational journalism.

Further definition of policy as to *The Journal* is to be found in the report of the editorial department, for 1921-1922: [7]

> The following types of material are described in the approximate order of their claim for inclusion. [In the opinion of the Editorial Council.] [8]
>
> 1. Official accounts of the association's work, and editorials designed to further its program.
> 2. Material related to the organization and work of teachers' associations generally, more especially of state and local affiliated associations.
> 3. Accounts of educational legislation, administration, policies, plans, and scientific advance, thus making the best experience quickly available.
> 4. Material which, because of the peculiar position of *The Journal*, it can better publish than any other periodical. It should give special consideration to new movements in education and to matters of national and international concern which should be brought quickly to the attention of members.

A somewhat more aggressive policy is implied in the report of the Division of Publications for the following year: [9] "An educational journal may build itself around the manuscripts that come voluntarily to it, or it may assume a creative attitude and reach out to stimulate thinking along educational lines by asking for articles on special subjects. The second plan is the aim of *The Journal*."

A year later in the division's report emphasis was put upon limitations which should be recognized in determining the proper functions of *The Journal:* [10]

> The primary duty [of *The Journal*] is to deal with the broader problems of education which affect all teachers alike and which are vitally related to the welfare of the nation and its children. . . . [*The Journal* should not be departmentalized, as its contents would then be] a collection of special appeals. . . . No material should go into *The Journal* [which is not] in entire

---

[6] *Add. and Proc.*, 1921, pp. 211-12.
[7] *Add. and Proc.*, 1922, p. 133.
[8] An advisory committee of members of the association.
[9] *Add. and Proc.*, 1923, p. 113.
[10] *Add. and Proc.*, 1924, pp. 121-22.

Activities and Objectives

accord with the association's adopted policies as indicated by the minutes of the Representative Assembly and other bodies. The Journal does not aim primarily to express the views of the editor, of the Editorial Council, or of the other officers. It is the official mouthpiece of our association, which has a recognized program. By promoting this program *The Journal* can render its greatest service to the profession.

[It will not include methods and devices nor classroom material, but will leave this field to private educational periodicals.]

It cannot deal in personal compliment and praise and in certain materials of local appeal. . . . Every item that is included must meet the test of its interest to the whole profession and its intrinsic merit as a suggestion to educational workers throughout the country in the improvement of professional practice.

A more positive note is sounded in the 1926 report: [11]

In the plans [of *The Journal*] for 1926-27, a considerable portion of each number is built around the idea, "The Professional at Work on Its Problems." There have been selected for special emphasis, (1) scientific contributions to the new curriculum, (2) character and the school, and (3) building beauty into everyday life.

[There will also be reports of new books and educational statistics.]

Further evidence as to policy is to be found in the division's report for 1927-1928, in which it is recorded that *The Journal* published in that year a series of articles on careers in education, showing opportunities in education as a life career, with statements of training needed. It published, also, a series of articles on Growth in the Educational Service, designed for use in faculty meetings; reported statistics showing "needs and achievements of the schools"; sought to make more effective "interpretive projects like American Education Week, vitalized commencements, opportunities in summer schools, and the annual roll call of progress"; secured judgments from readers as to most helpful features.[12]

The Journal continues to be printed on quarto size paper. Since January, 1922 it has contained sixty-four pages, in addition to cover pages, from thirty to forty per cent of the space being used by advertisers. It is printed on white paper, with cover of ivory color. The staff attempts to make it attractive by the generous use of boxes and half-tones. It is printed monthly, from October to June, inclusive, and is distributed by mail to all members of the association. It is the only means of intra-group communication that reaches the whole group.

[11] *Add. and Proc.*, 1926, pp. 1149-50.
[12] *Annual Report of the Secretary*, as presented at Minneapolis, Minnesota, July, 1928, pp. 32-33.

3. *Publicity.* In addition to its function of intra-group communication, the Division of Publications carries on extra-group communication. It reported in 1921 [13] that releases consisting of advance copies of editorials, programs, and copies of addresses delivered at convention sessions had been sent to 100 educational journals; and that releases covering teacher shortage, the salary situation, the Education Bill and the association's meetings had been sent to 1,500 press syndicates and daily newspapers. Releases were sent out to members, or with membership invitations to non-members, to be given to local editors.

Conferences were held with local newspaper representatives in Des Moines prior to the 1921 convention, for the purpose of explaining the association and the arrangement of its meetings and emphasizing the importance of educational news.[14]

In 1923, it was reported that the division had been attempting to get newspapers and magazines to feature education on their own initiative. In connection with conventions, publicity had been provided not only through newspapers and magazines but by means of the radio and motion pictures as well.[15]

In 1925, the director said:

> To arouse interest in education among editors of newspapers and magazines and influential citizens is the central aim of the association's publicity. Its contacts include educational journals, daily newspapers, press associations, feature writers, magazine editors, women's magazines, the religious press, agricultural press, business magazines, foreign periodicals, public men, and the journals of organized labor. . . . Radio broadcasting has come directly into use in the association's meetings.[16]

In 1928, a new method of publicity was reported:

> Each week during the year the division has furnished through the Associated Press to twelve hundred daily newspapers a special feature service. These weekly articles have dealt with important questions in education and have been written by prominent members of the profession.[17]

How these educational feature articles are prepared is told in the typewritten "Plan for Interpreting the Schools to the Public Through the Associated Press." [18]

[13] *Add. and Proc., 1921*, p. 237.
[14] *Add. and Proc., 1922*, p. 137.
[15] *Add. and Proc., 1923*, pp. 115-17.
[16] *Add. and Proc., 1925*, p. 1041.
[17] *Annual Report of the Secretary*, Minneapolis, Minnesota, July, 1928, p. 33.
[18] Furnished by the Division of Publications.

Activities and Objectives

1. Members of the National Education Association's headquarters staff, many of whom are specialists in particular fields, are constantly in touch with significant problems of forward movements in American Education. The staff members report such problems or movements, together with names of persons who are prominently identified with them, to the Division of Publications.

2. The Secretary of the association is consulted on the selection of subjects and authors invited to contribute to the series and the invitations are issued by the Division of Publications.

3. In the invitations to prospective authors it is explained that, from the standpoint of the National Education Association, the purpose of the educational series is twofold; first, to acquaint the public with reliable information and, second, to familiarize the people of America with the nation's largest professional organization—the National Education Association. Writers of the articles are requested if it is convenient, to mention the name of the association.

4. A photograph of the author accompanies each article.

These articles are approximately 350 words in length, and are written in newspaper English. Inspection of a large collection of them reveals very little direct promotion of the National Education Association as an organization. Apparently the aims are to make the teacher appear human, to make his work appear important, to cite instances of his devotion to his work, to report new features of school activity—in general, to inform the population at large in regard to its schools and its teachers and to develop a favorable social attitude toward them; to improve the social situation in which the teacher works.

Titles of the first twenty-four articles in the series were as follows:

1. Salaries of College Teachers
2. The Adult Illiterate
3. The Opening of Schools
4. The Principal Talks to Parents
5. Health of the Preschool Child
6. What the Rural School Needs Most
7. Character Education
8. The Schools of Yesterday and To-day
9. Summer Schools Enrollment of Teachers
10. Mechanical Ability Tests
11. Teacher Training
12. Recreation in Lincoln School
13. The Schools and Public Goodwill
14. What Is Done in a Modern School System
15. The Public School as a Trainer of Home Makers
16. The School Drum Corps and the Problem Boy
17. Summer Camp for High School Musicians

18. The Development of Character Through Work
19. All Year Schools
20. The Super-Bright Child
21. One-Talent Children
22. The Cleveland College Journalism Course
23. The Newspaper and the School
24. The Educational Outlook for 1928

The "press service" at conventions is described by the Division of Publications as follows: [19]

> The growing importance of National Education Association conventions has led to an interest manifest by the profession and laity throughout the country. Every convention held in an important center of population attracts representatives of many magazines and metropolitan dailies, sent to report for their readers the events of the meetings. A convention has on its program so many sessions that a single person is never able to attend more than a small portion of them.
>
> Therefore, it has become necessary to establish a clearing agency whose workers are familiar with the association and also with the entire convention and who have on file reports of as many as possible of the addresses delivered at the convention. To meet that need the Division of Publications of the National Education Association has been charged with the responsibility of maintaining the "N. E. A. Press Service" at all winter and summer conventions.
>
> PREPARATIONS FOR CONVENTION PUBLICITY—SUMMARIES OF ADDRESSES
>
> (a) Six weeks before the convention is to begin, a multigraphed circular letter is sent from the Division of Publications to each speaker on the convention program. This letter calls attention to the magnitude of the convention, and the importance of having it well presented to the public through newspapers and magazines. It asks each speaker to send a 300-word summary of his address to the office of the Division of Publications not later than three weeks before the opening of the convention; to leave a copy of the summary with each newspaper in his home city; and to leave with the secretary of the meeting at which he speaks a complete copy of the address. A sample 300-word newspaper summary of a convention address is inclosed with the letter.
>
> (b) Three weeks later a second or "follow-up" letter is sent to all speakers in order that those who have not yet sent their speech summaries will do so as early as possible. . . .
>
> (c) The 300-word summaries of convention addresses, as rapidly as they are received in the Washington office, are edited to conform to newspaper style and are mimeographed. . . .
>
> (d) Copies of the mimeographed summaries are sent immediately to national news-distributing agencies, for example, The Associated Press, The International News Service, The United Press Association.

[19] In a typewritten handbook personally furnished by the division.

Activities and Objectives

(e) For four weeks before the convention opens press releases are sent to newspapers in the convention state, and to all newspapers in the United States having special education departments.

(f) Two weeks preceding the convention a letter of information is sent to the news staff of each newspaper in the convention city. This letter gives briefly a statement of the work and purpose of the association, gives the names of officers and members of the headquarters staff, and describes their duties. Newspaper writers are easily confused in handling names and initials of a large group of people. The letters aim to minimize the possibility of such errors.

(g) Newspapers in the convention city are supplied with such advance photographs or additional information as they may request by mail.

(h) A planographed "broadside" showing clippings from newspapers at former conventions is sent to newspapers in the convention city to acquaint its writers with the nature of the meeting and the type of press mention it merits. . . .

DUTIES OF THE NATIONAL EDUCATION ASSOCIATION PRESS SERVICE AT CONVENTIONS

(a) Before the convention opens. The work of the National Education Association press service in the convention city actually begins from four days to a week before the convention opens, with the arrival of the director and other assigned members of the Division of Publications. It is customary for the director or another member of the staff to make immediate personal contact with the city editor of each local newspaper and with the local correspondent of the Associated Press.

In some convention cities newspaper editors ask representatives of the association to address the news staff members on the significance of the convention. It is advisable to make contacts with local news agencies through the city school official who is most intimately in touch with the press.

With the aid of the National Education Association press service newspapers are able to publish advance news items describing the convention "set-up" and forecasting outstanding events to take place on the program. . . .

At least three days before the convention begins the National Education Association press service office is definitely opened and typists are set to work making copies of late releases and of other material for newspaper use.

(b) During the convention. The office of the National Education Association press service is completely staffed and equipped, with every worker familiar with his duties on the opening day of the convention. . . .[20]

4. *Proceedings.* The Division of Publications is in charge of the publication of the annual volumes of *Addresses and Proceedings.* These are octavo volumes, from approximately 700 to somewhat more than 1,500 pages in length (1922). In recent years, they have been kept uniformly at approximately 1,200 pages. These volumes

---

[20] A staff of fifteen or more persons is employed.

contain a record of the addresses delivered at the general sessions of the annual convention and at the sessions of the departments as well;[21] names of officers; reports of committees, with names of committee members; records of sessions of the Representative Assembly, with a roster of names of delegates; a copy of the Act of Incorporation and of the by-laws of the association; minutes of the meetings of the Board of Directors and of the Executive Committee; treasurer's and auditor's reports; budget report; secretary's report. The *Addresses and Proceedings* circulate largely through libraries, although a few members purchase them for themselves.[22] These volumes in their printed form are to be classed as historic records of the group, not as communication. The materials included are assembled, arranged, abstracted, edited, sent to authors for approval, and proofread by the Division of Publications.[23]

5. *Other Publications.* In addition to *The Journal* and the *Addresses and Proceedings*, there are numerous publications issued or "cleared" through this division.[24] These include publications of the departments, programs of conventions, research bulletins, American Education Week bulletins, and other materials of considerable variety.[25] The division's functions with regard to these materials are editorial and supervisory.

This division is a complex agency of communication. It is complex, not only because it is concerned with both intra- and extra-group communication, and with historic records as well as current materials, but also because of the variety of methods which it uses.

There is no record of the effectiveness of intra-group communication achieved by *The Journal*—the principal means in use. It is impossible within the scope of this study to determine what kinds or what amounts of the published materials are read by the members, or what their influence is on appreciations, loyalties, oppositions, coöperations, thought. The fact that an attempt is made to include only such material as will be of interest to all classes of teachers may mean that there is no great intensity or quantity of practical professional value for any particular class of members. On the other hand, a kind of value different from the immediately practical is undoubtedly attached to the individual member's receipt and

[21] Many of the addresses are printed in abridged form.
[22] The circulation of these volumes was reported in 1924 to be from 5,000 to 7,500. *Add. and Proc.*, 1924, p. 1041.
[23] *Add. and Proc.*, 1921, p. 237.
[24] *Add. and Proc.*, 1926, p. 1144.
[25] *Add. and Proc.*, 1922, p. 136.

Activities and Objectives

possession of an official medium of group communication. Such a periodical is the objective symbol of group contact, group membership, group participation, and as such it has value, regardless of the fact that the definitely practical material in it may be small in amount.

A careful analysis of the actual contents of *The Journal* from the time of its establishment through 1928 shows that it is engaged in the following activities or functions: [26]

1. It informs members about the association itself and about its departments: convention dates and places and programs; efforts to secure legislation; conferences held; resolutions adopted; size of membership; proposed changes in organization.
2. It gives information about teachers' welfare: reports of salary levels, tenure laws, retirement provisions, qualifications for appointment, summer school attendance.
3. It furnishes occupational aids or service: selected lists of professional and other books; guides to professional study programs; patriotic and other special materials; discussions of child health, school clubs, school buildings, special schools, safety education, recreation, textbook selection, school taxes, the curriculum.
4. It promotes membership drives through publication of lists of 100 per cent schools, lists of life members, pleas to readers (members) to secure other members.
5. It gives public recognition to members and leaders by publishing quotations from their addresses and writings; by publishing their photographs, and photographs of their projects; by laudatory comments concerning them.
6. It "inspires" its readers, increases their self-esteem, raises their feeling of status, by asserting the connection of teaching with the maintenance of moretic values.
7. It presents statements of interpretation of the association's stand on issues.

[26] A quantitative analysis of the contents of *The Journal*, by columns, for example, would probably not yield any significant result, that is, a result capable of interpretation, because of the multiplicity of factors entering into the make-up of such a periodical. In the absence of standards for determining the relative "impressiveness" of long and short articles, boxed and plain composition, front page and later page, large type and small type, *etc.*, any kind of classification except on the basis of intended function—showing what the editor and others evidently intend to communicate to the membership—is probably valueless.

8. It discusses general social problems in which teachers are known to be interested, for example, international peace, child labor, etc.
9. It stimulates group thought along selected professional lines by securing writers to contribute articles along these lines, for example, in the series of articles entitled, "Growth in the Educational Service" in 1927-1928.

It should be noted that no adverse criticism of the association in any of its aspects is included in *The Journal*. It informs the members about the association and interprets its policies to them, always favorably. The intention of the leaders obviously is that *The Journal* should not be a forum for free discussion of association affairs but merely an agency of communication to report what the leaders wish to report to the membership. Whether this is a sound policy may well be questioned.[27] It may have the immediate effect of keeping down internal opposition and avoiding division, but in the long run the unity which is achieved through a stifling or limiting of discussion is insecurely based. Certainly this is true for purely voluntary membership groups such as the National Education Association in which all the members may be assumed to be intelligent, and many of them broadly trained along general and professional lines. If free and open competition of ideas has value in any society in separating truth from error it would have value in a group such as this. Serious group weakness or error or shortsightedness may be present even at a time of apparent group success, if channels of communication are open only for discussion favorable to current policy and practice. An organization's longtime advancement, if it is to be assured, must be based upon critically analyzed, sound principles. The association could lose nothing, and it might gain much, by letting *The Journal* be used for free discussion of present and future policies.

Of course, there are other channels through which association affairs are subjected to more or less criticism. At the annual convention, delegates to the Representative Assembly engage in untrammeled discussion. But, as pointed out elsewhere in this study,[28] the convention time limits, the size of the group, the differences in convention experience and in prestige of delegates, and in general the crowd situation all render the assembly an ineffective body for delib-

[27] Ross, E. A., *Principles of Sociology*, Chap. XXIII.
[28] Chap. V.

Activities and Objectives

eration and reasoned judgment. However, if prior to the convention there had been pro and con discussion in the columns of *The Journal* of issues to be presented to the assembly for decision, so that delegates and their constituents might have given them careful consideration, there would be much less reason to object to the pronouncements made by the assembly as being typical crowd products.

Another channel for criticism of association policies is the educational press. But no one periodical reaches all association members, hence intra-group communication through this channel is imperfect. Moreover, discussion of the association is of only incidental concern to a privately owned periodical, hence would tend to be intermittent and incomplete, and biased by the special objectives of each periodical. Such discussions as do appear in these publications, whether adverse or favorable to current association activities, might properly be reported to the membership through *The Journal* itself in line with the policy here proposed of keeping the members informed so that they can act intelligently.

The varieties and amounts of publicity or extra-group communication have increased greatly since 1921. Although there is no record to show how much newspaper and magazine space is devoted to accounts of the annual conventions, nor how many of the 1,200 newspapers use the articles written for the feature service, nor how many persons read them when they are printed, nor how many persons are reached by radio addresses, nor what the reaction is to any of these, the techniques and plans used are such as are likely to result in effective communication: [29]

1. The function of extra-group communication has been delegated largely to a specialized subgroup employed for performing this function.
2. Definite programs of publicity are adopted and systematically carried out.
3. The merit of indirect suggestion [30] is recognized in that an effort is made to interest editors and influential citizens in the activities and program of the association in the expectation that these persons will in turn communicate to other non-members

---

[29] Kulp, D. H., II, *Outlines of the Sociology of Human Behavior*, Chaps. LI, XXVIII, XXXIV.
Park, R. E. and Burgess, E. W., *Introduction to the Science of Sociology*, pp. 315-17; 356-89.
[30] Sidis, B., *The Psychology of Suggestion*, p. 52.

of the association and of the teaching profession the suggestions which the association has communicated to them.
4. Rapport between the association and the personnel of the newspaper staff in the convention city is fostered by the use of an intermediate contact agent who is well known to both groups, namely, a local school official who has a close relationship with the press.
5. Much of the effort to establish extra-group communication is concentrated at times and in geographic areas in which it is most likely to be effective, namely, near and at the time of the conventions, in and near the convention cities. Traditions of hospitality, commercial interest, activity in providing places of meeting, journalistic enterprise, popular interest in the near-at-hand, all combine to create a situation in which the reaction to communication is likely to be positive and favorable.
6. In order that communication may not be hindered by a universe of discourse divergent from the colloquial, feature articles are written in "newspaper style."
7. Many of those whose contributed articles or abridged addresses are sent out to the newspapers, or who speak over the radio, are persons of considerable prestige.[31] The personal prestige of the association's spokesmen increases the importance attached to the communications on the part of non-members.

The preservation of the *Addresses and Proceedings* in printed form is of great sociological importance. It is not so effective as other means of communication within the present association or between the association and other groups, because of the limited general circulation of these volumes. But because there is recorded in this series of volumes the only relatively complete account of what is said and done by the leaders at the annual meetings of the association, it becomes probably the best means of communication between the present and succeeding groups of leaders, and provides a basis for historical continuity.[32]

The Research Division. This division was organized March 1, 1922. It began immediately to function as a specialized fact-finding and fact-furnishing agency, serving the various committees and commissions of the association that had investigations under way, and even attempting to supply information on miscellaneous matters to

[31] Hayes, E. C., *Introduction to the Study of Sociology*, Chap. XVIII.
[32] Park and Burgess, *op. cit.*, pp. 283-84.

individual members upon request. Its findings were at first published at irregular intervals but since January, 1923, it has issued a *Research Bulletin* of 32 to 132 pages, octavo size, regularly five times each year, in addition to occasional special publications. It also publishes in *The Journal* at least one page per month of statistical tabulations and a limited number of interpretative articles, this material dealing with matters thought to be of interest to the whole membership.

The annual report of the division in 1924 [33] states its objectives as follows:

1. Conduct studies vital to the improvement of public school legislation and financial support.
2. Furnish information to association members and affiliated organizations for use in advancing the welfare of the teaching profession.
3. Coördinate the research work of the association's committees and departments.
4. Supply special material needed by the association's headquarters staff.
5. Serve as a clearing house for studies in the field of educational research.
6. Collect and disseminate current facts for the promotion of education.
7. Fill each issue of the *Research Bulletin* of the National Education Association with timely information.

These statements have been amplified in other reports and discussions to include serving the committees and departments and divisions instead of simply coördinating their work; preparing "readable articles based on exact data" (1923); acting "as a general service agency to state and local teachers organizations and to individual members of the organization" (1925); developing a service for "summarizing and synthesizing the results of educational research" (1926).

The practice seems increasingly to be for the committees and commissions that are established both by the association itself and by its departments to determine the scope of the investigations which they wish to carry on, and then to turn to the Division of Research to secure the essential data and to present the data in such form

[33] *Add. and Proc.*, 1924, pp. 124-25.

that interpretation is easy.³⁴ The range of subjects investigated and reported is, therefore, at least as wide as that in which the association by its creation of committees and commissions has shown interest. The division's work, however, is not limited to serving these special interest groups. It undertakes investigations on its own account and publishes its findings, thus assuming a leadership rôle as well as a service rôle.

Since its establishment it has engaged in the following activities: It has either independently or in coöperation with a subgroup, assembled and published data on many phases of the welfare of teachers: salary, tenure, retirement, training requirements, married women teachers, examination for appointment, leave of absence, sick leave. It has supplied extensive information on curricula and on school costs. It has reported consensus of opinion on bibliographies. It has compiled general information of interest to teachers, such as facts concerning the growth of parent-teacher associations, the size of summer schools, illiteracy, wealth of states, educational opportunity in different areas, legislation, school results. It has furnished practical professional information on such topics as prevailing practices in administration and supervision and time allotments for subjects. It has formulated and published standards and principles related to education in its various aspects.

The *Research Bulletin* for September, 1922 (Vol. I, No. 4), offers a good case illustration of the two general functions performed by this division: information service and propaganda.³⁵ This number bears the title: "Five Questions for American Education Week." The first question, "What are the weak spots in our public school system?" is answered, or material is furnished for answering it, in twelve tables, with captions as follows:

Table 1. State Compulsory School Attendance Laws
Table 2. Cost of Education in One-Room School and Graded School
Table 3. Are All Children in Your State Attending School?
Table 4. Is the One-Room School Costly?
Table 5. What Progress Has Been Made in Your State in Replacing the Costly One-Room School with Consolidated Graded Schools?
Table 6. Are the Children of Your State Taught by Trained Teachers?
Table 7. What Experience and Maturity Have the Teachers in the Rural Schools of Your State?

---

³⁴ See p. 53 of the present study.

³⁵ By propaganda is meant simply the use of techniques of communication that persuade and convince as different from those that merely inform. (See Kulp, D. H., II, *op. cit.,* Chap. LI.)

Activities and Objectives

Table 8. Are Salaries in Your State Such That You Can Expect Competent Teachers in All Classrooms?
Table 9. Are All American Children Given Equal School Opportunities?
Table 10. Growth in Value of Physical Property, National Income, and Public School Expenditures
Table 11. Is the Percentage of School Money Raised in the Local Community Too Great in Your State?
Table 12. Are Too Many School Children in Your State on Part-Time Attendance?

The second question, "What national defects result from the weak spots in our public school system?" is answered by data tabulated as follows:

Table 13. How Many Child Laborers in Your State Are Being Denied School Opportunities?
Table 14. Illiteracy in the United States and Foreign Countries
Table 15. Increase in the Number of Illiterates in Twelve States
Table 16. Are There Too Many Illiterates in Your State?
Table 17. Federal Census and Army Draft Illiteracy
Table 18. Are There Too Many Native-Born Illiterates in Your State?
Table 19. How Many Foreign-Born Residents Has Your State?
Table 20. Percentage of Illiteracy in Countries from Which Nearly Half Our 14,000,000 Foreign-Born Came
Table 21. How Many Native-Born Adult Illiterates Are There in Your State?
Table 22. Rejections for Physical Disabilities and Casualties, U. S. Army, World War
Table 23. Does the Physical Condition of the Men of Your State Qualify Them for the Duties of Peace?

The third question, "How may our public school system be strengthened?" is answered in wholly different fashion. There are no tables but there is a series of dogmatic statements in bold-faced type, followed by discussion and explanation, a clear instance of intra-group communication and extra-group propaganda:

1. The people through a state law should require all schools to be open at least eight months each year.
2. The people through a state law should require full-time attendance of all children of school age.
3. The people through a state-wide census should provide for the proper accounting of the greatest of their natural resources, their children.
4. The people through a state law should guarantee all children instruction from trained and capable teachers.
5. The people through a state law should require all schools to meet certain standards, such as conducting all classes in the English language.
6. The people through an adequate State Equalization Fund should make

it possible for all local districts, without levying an unreasonably high tax, to maintain a school that meets all state requirements.

7. The State School Equalization Fund should be distributed among the local districts in a manner that guarantees every American boy and girl an educational opportunity.
8. The people through the state should maintain an efficient State Department of Education.
9. All citizens should keep themselves informed as to conditions in their [local] schools.
10. Careful discrimination should be used in voting for members of the school board.
11. See that a careful plan is in effect for the selection and retention of capable teachers.
12. School boards should adopt a salary schedule that will attract and hold capable teachers.
13. Capable teachers and school officials should be guaranteed tenure in office.
14. The people should consolidate those school districts that are too small to maintain a modern school.
15. Every community should have a carefully planned school building program.[36]

To answer question four, "Can the nation afford an adequate school system?" there is a return to the presentation of tabulated data:

Table 24. The Nation's Wealth and Educational Expenditures
Table 25. National Income and School Costs
Table 26. Educational Expenditures and Other Expenditures in 1920
Table 27. Estimated Annual Expenditures for Luxuries, 1920

The final question, "Do good schools pay?" is also answered by the assembling of facts:

Table 28. School Efficiency and Literacy
Table 29. School Efficiency 1900 and Literary Digest Circulation 1922
Table 30. Public School Efficiency, General Level of Educational Attainment and Information on Public Questions
Table 31. Public School Efficiency and General Intelligence
Table 32. Public School Efficiency and the Production of Men and Women of Leadership
Table 33. Public School Efficiency, General Intelligence, and Leadership in National Affairs
Table 34. School Efficiency and Earning Power
Table 35. School Efficiency as Measured by Savings Deposits
Table 36. Public School Efficiency, Earning Power, and Thrift

[36] These direct suggestions undoubtedly gain in effectiveness from the fact of their proximity to statistical tabulations. This proximity constitutes an indirect suggestion that the statements are a product of similar tabulations.

Activities and Objectives 115

The Research Division, in its fact-finding and fact-furnishing activities, is to be classified as a service agency. It gathers information from primary and secondary sources and arranges and summarizes it in standardized tabular form so that it can be used by members of the National Education Association and by local and state associations of teachers and by committees of the National Education Association in intra-group discussion and in extra-group propaganda. When the division does more than assemble and interpret data, when it makes general applications of its findings to problems, or when it includes, as part of its reports the application of general principles or standards, even though these may be very widely accepted, then it itself becomes an agency of communication and of propaganda.[37]

The creation of this division, its expansion, and the fact that committees and commissions of the association increasingly utilize its fact-finding services in carrying on their study of their special problems (as discussed elsewhere in this study)—these are conclusive evidences that the association is making progress in the use of the objective, statistical methods of science.

A very practical problem for the association to face is that of determining what particular researches to undertake, for obviously the number of possible studies in the field of education is legion. Since this is a general and national body, any educational issue may be attacked with propriety. Since the funds available are not unlimited, selection must be made. In the absence of techniques for determining what studies to make and in what order, there is the possibility that energy and money may be expended with somewhat less than maximum value to the association as a whole or to the educational profession. There is one function which only such an association as this or a government agency like the Office of Education is likely to undertake because of its size and general character, namely, "summarizing and synthesizing the results of educational research." This the association now apparently means to do.[38] This kind of activity, it would seem, should have a claim upon the resources of the Research Division ahead of that of any other project, for it is not only poor economy on the part of the association, but it is poor general social economy to risk duplication of investigation at a time when so many educational problems have not been

---

[37] See footnote 35, p. 112 of the present study.
[38] See p. 111 of the present study.

investigated at all. If this summarizing and synthesizing service were performed, the division might very naturally be recognized as a proper coördinator of future educational researches undertaken by various independent agencies. The professional gain from such coordination would be enormous.

Division of Classroom Service. This division, called at first the Division of Elementary School Service, was created in September, 1922, "for the purpose of giving assistance to the classroom teachers of the country either through their organizations or individually when such help is desired." [39]

According to the annual reports of the division, the director has acted as headquarters secretary for those of the departments that are not primarily interested in administrative problems and for several organizations allied with the association. The division has devoted much time to assisting the Department of Classroom Teachers, especially in recent years, in the editing of its yearbook and its news bulletin. It has gathered information as to the activities of local affiliated organizations of classroom teachers and passed this information on to other groups. At one time it took a referendum in a large number of such organizations to discover "the problems which they would like to see worked out." Much of the work of preparing the program of the annual convention and of coördinating it with the programs of departments and allied organizations has been done by this division. It has given special attention to providing articles in *The Journal* that are of interest to classroom teachers. It has contributed articles on the association to the *New Americana Annual* and to *The World Almanac,* and has prepared a monthly press release consisting of brief excerpts from *The Journal.* It has maintained a general information service.

It is clear that this division is not so completely specialized in its activities as are the others. Its director might well bear the title of assistant secretary. However, it is perhaps not inappropriate to include these non-specialized functions under the very general head of classroom service.

Division of Administrative Service. This division always bears a double name in the annual reports of the headquarters staff: The Department of Superintendence and Division of Administrative Service. Its head is given the double title of executive secretary of the department and director of the division. In the capacity of director,

[39] *Add. and Proc.,* 1923, p. 122.

this officer cares for the interests of the departments that are primarily concerned with questions of administration, for example, the Department of Elementary School Principals, and for those of other organizations related to the Department of Superintendence, either in convention planning or by common interest. "Convention details for the fourteen allied organizations which coöperate with the Department of Superintendence in the winter meeting are handled by this division. An extensive information service is maintained for individual school administrators as well as for organizations, local, state, and national, interested in administrative questions." [40]

An Educational Research Service is maintained in coöperation with the Research Division. This is made self-supporting through the collection of an annual fee of $25 from each school system that subscribes.

> This service is intended to provide a clearing-house by which subscribers may be informed of studies actual and proposed by various research agencies. Subscribers are furnished with printed or multigraphed copies of studies not available for general distribution prepared by cities, universities, and societies. . . . An effort has been made to work out some practical solution of the questionnaire problem.[41]

This division is a somewhat highly specialized service agency. It does not directly serve the association as a whole, but only such subgroups as are interested in administration, and primarily the one subgroup, the Department of Superintendence. Even though it serves the general association only indirectly, its service may be none the less valuable. The arrangement by which an executive division of the association and the executive office of a department are combined prevents overlapping of effort and provides for complete coördination. There seems to be no reason why this arrangement might not be made between the association and other departments.

[40] *Add. and Proc.*, 1926, p. 1159.
[41] *Add. and Proc.*, 1926, p. 1158.

CHAPTER VII

ACTIVITIES AND OBJECTIVES (*Concluded*)

THE REPRESENTATIVE ASSEMBLY

The activities of the Representative Assembly are very briefly defined in the by-laws as "the election of officers and the transaction of business" (Article II, Section 1). "Transaction of business" is vague. An adequate idea of the functioning of this body can be gained only by a rather complete listing of the different kinds of action taken in the annual meetings at the time of the summer convention, as recorded in the minutes of the meetings. The list given in the next paragraph is believed to include the significant *kinds* of action taken from 1922 to 1928, inclusive, naming each activity only once, even though some were repeated several times.

During this period the Representative Assembly, functioning collectively, has engaged in the following activities:

1. Creating committees
2. Receiving reports of committees
3. Discontinuing committees
4. Electing officers (including each year a trustee and a member of the Executive Committee)
5. Receiving reports of officers
6. Receiving reports of Board of Trustees
7. Receiving reports of Executive Committee
8. Receiving reports of Board of Directors
9. Acting on proposed amendments to by-laws
10. Acting on payment of delegates' expenses
11. Creating new departments
12. Discussing activities of departments
13. Discontinuing departments
14. Receiving report of proceedings of World Federation of Education Associations
15. Voting to join World Federation of Education Associations
16. Hearing prepared addresses on topics of professional and association interest
17. Instructing headquarters divisions
18. Adopting resolution of appreciation and confidence in secretary of association

Activities and Objectives

19. Presenting banner to state delegations for best membership records
20. Directing that inquiry be made as to reported dismissal of teachers because of membership in National Education Association
21. Sending greetings to teachers of Belgium
22. Sending greetings to National Association of Teachers in Colored Schools
23. Sending greetings to President of the United States
24. Receiving greetings from National Editorial Association
25. Receiving greetings from National Association of Teachers in Colored Schools
26. Receiving greetings from Lithuanian representative
27. Receiving greetings from Chilean representative
28. Receiving greetings from president of Japanese Education Association
29. Receiving greetings from Hawaiian delegation
30. Receiving greetings from the German Teachers Association
31. Receiving greetings from Near East Relief children

In addition to the foregoing activites which may be considered to represent the primary functionings of this body, others are engaged in incidentally. It is of importance to list these because they indicate something as to the mood or tone of the sessions. These include:

1. Repeating the Lord's Prayer in unison. (At some conventions, this is part of the formality of opening each day's session. It seems not to be firmly established as a custom, however, for it is sometimes omitted.)
2. Listening to prayer by clergyman. (In place of repetition of Lord's Prayer. Sometimes, however, both are omitted.)
3. Standing silently in honor of "educational pioneers." (This has occurred once only, and this impulsively at the suggestion of an older member.)
4. Listening to state songs and demonstrations (limited usually to state delegations seeking next convention).
5. Applauding. (Praise of leader, such as president or secretary, brings applause, as does also the expression, by any speaker, of stereotyped educational or patriotic sentiments.) [1]

BOARD OF DIRECTORS

The Act of Incorporation provides (Section 6):

The Board of Directors shall have power to fill all vacancies in their own body; shall have in charge the general interests of the corporation, excepting those herein intrusted to the Board of Trustees; and shall possess such other powers as shall be conferred upon them by the by-laws of the corporation.

The by-laws (Article III, Section 4) enumerate the following specific obligations of the Board of Directors:

1. To elect corresponding members
2. To elect members of the National Council of Education

[1] Cf. Lippmann, Walter, *Public Opinion*, Chaps. VI, VII, X.

3. To fill vacancies in its own body and in the Board of Trustees
4. To approve bills incurred by itself or by the Executive Committee, or by the president or secretary when authorized to act for the board
5. To make necessary appropriations as ordered by the Representative Assembly
6. To make a full report of the financial condition of the association, including reports of Secretary, Treasurer, and Board of Trustees, to Representative Assembly
7. To "do all in its power to make the association a useful and honorable institution."

Examination of the minutes of the Board of Directors from 1922 to 1928 shows that this body has engaged in the following kinds of activities, each kind being listed only once:

1. Receiving report of Secretary
2. Receiving report of Treasurer
3. Receiving report of Board of Trustees
4. Receiving report of Executive Committee
5. Discussing report prepared by Executive Committee for Representative Assembly
6. Appointing auditing committee
7. Approving budget prepared by Executive Committee
8. Creating a department
9. Discontinuing a department
10. Merging two departments
11. Rejecting application for new department
12. Authorizing Executive Committee to take action on departments
13. Changing name of department
14. Electing member of Board of Trustees
15. Accepting resignation of member of Board of Trustees
16. Electing member of Executive Committee
17. Electing members of National Council
18. Electing corresponding member of association
19. Electing directors to fill vacancies
20. Accepting resignations of State Directors and electing persons nominated by those withdrawing
21. Accepting resignations of those representing directors and reinstating those regularly elected
22. Taking vote of preference as to place of next convention, for guidance of Executive Committee
23. Choosing convention city
24. Authorizing Executive Committee to fix time of convention
25. Approving purchase of additional property subject to decision of Board of Trustees
26. Creating committees to study revision of departments, payment of delegates' expenses, conferring of honorary degrees by association, all-inclusive membership, and other matters affecting the organization

Activities and Objectives

27. Receiving reports of board's own committees and of committees of the association
28. Recommending creation of association committees
29. Enacting rule as to time of presenting credentials by delegates to Representative Assembly
30. Approving plans and committee appointments of president
31. Hearing a plan for enlisting the laity in support of education
32. Discussing "attacks made during the year on the association and its officers"
33. Authorizing Executive Committee to act in budget matters for Board of Directors
34. Approving action of Executive Committee in matters affecting headquarters staff
35. Giving Executive Committee full authority and responsibility for policies and plans of *The Journal* and other publications, including style and spelling
36. Authorizing Executive Committee to act for Board of Directors between sessions
37. Discussing needed simplification of auditors' report
38. Recommending change in method of electing directors
39. Appropriating money for committees
40. Establishing policy of having association pay directors' expenses
41. Appropriating money for payment of directors' expenses
42. Recommending appropriation for part payment of delegates' expenses
43. Considering question of utilities corporations' propaganda in schools
44. Listening to representatives of National Electric Light Association on question of propaganda in schools
45. Deciding to adopt the National Education Association emblem and colors

EXECUTIVE COMMITTEE

The Act of Incorporation makes brief reference to the functions of this body, stating merely (Section 6) that it "shall have authority to represent, and to act for the Board of Directors in the intervals between the meetings of that body, to the extent of carrying out the legislation adopted by the Board of Directors under general directions as may be given by said board."

The by-laws (Article III, Section 5) state that this committee *may* recommend to the Representative Assembly the appointment of committees and that it *shall* perform the following functions:

1. Recommend the appropriation of money for committees
2. Supervise committees
3. Receive, consider, print and present (to the Board of Directors) reports of committees, Secretary, Treasurer, Board of Trustees, these to be transmitted to the Representative Assembly
4. Fill "vacancies occurring in the body of officers of the association. . . ."

These brief provisions give a very inadequate idea of the great variety of activities to be found recorded in the minutes. The Executive Committee meets at least twice each year, at the time of the annual convention in the summer and again in connection with the meeting of the Department of Superintendence. Occasionally, also, it meets in the autumn, at some convenient city, for example, in October, 1925, at Colorado Springs, and in September, 1926, at Chicago. A meeting is likely to continue for two or more days.

It apparently engages in practically all the activities of both the other bodies, and in some additional ones as well. Activities of a kind different from those undertaken by the larger bodies, as recorded in the minutes for 1922 to 1928, are as follows:

1. Creating a subcommittee to prepare the association's budget
2. Directing headquarters staff not to engage "in the political and partisan movements of the association"
3. Accepting resignation of member of headquarters staff
4. Fixing salaries of headquarters staff
5. Discussing railroad rates and service for convention
6. Fixing time and choosing place for convention
7. Accepting constitution and by-laws of new department
8. Receiving report of National Council of Education
9. Discussing detailed plans for improvement of headquarters building
10. Approving secretary's recommendation as to reassignment of rooms in headquarters building
11. Authorizing borrowing of funds when receipts are low
12. Hearing reports of heads of headquarters divisions
13. Transferring addressograph section from one headquarters division to another
14. Discussing the association's relationship to World Federation of Education Associations
15. Considering proposed constitution for World Federation of Education Associations
16. Making detailed arrangement for membership in World Federation of Education Associations
17. Joining American Council on Education
18. Voting to systematize payment of bills through standard voucher procedure
19. Providing for improved accounting system
20. Directing that simplified financial report to the association be provided
21. Discussing advertising rates in *The Journal*
22. Discussing use of cheaper paper in *The Journal*
23. Giving secretary veto power in policies of *The Journal*
24. Negotiating with National Association of Secondary School Principals about affiliation

Activities and Objectives

25. Accepting invitation to join Association for the Advancement of Science
26. Approving plan for accepting bequests
27. Discussing absences from duty on part of members of headquarters staff
28. Instructing secretary to hold copyright for association on published report of a committee
29. Limiting the uses of committee appropriations
30. Approving president's action in protesting attempt to oust a university chancellor
31. Discussing question of dismissal of superintendents and others engaged in school work
32. Making regulations concerning itemization of stenographic bills
33. Considering petition to make Research Division a clearing-house for educational research
34. Discussing advisability of accepting funds from private agencies and foundations
35. Voting to ask for place for member of association on convention program of American Federation of Labor
36. Authorizing coöperation with American Federation of Labor in preparation of platform for use of educational committees of labor unions
37. Authorizing printing of health charts
38. Authorizing printing of volume of poems selected by readers of *The Journal*, royalties to go to association
39. Authorizing selection of list of Classics for American Youth, with safeguards provided against commercial exploitation of the list
40. Directing that letter be written to a deposed teachers college president
41. Declaring election of two state directors for New York illegal
42. Authorizing conference of National Education Association leaders with state association representatives
43. Approving payment of life membership fee in ten installments
44. Letting contract for printing volume of *Addresses and Proceedings*
45. Adopting policy concerning commercial exhibits at conventions
46. Directing that Canadian teachers be invited as guests at convention
47. Appointing representatives to serve on board of directors and editorial board of *Encyclopedia of Social Sciences*
48. Considering endorsement of radio education program of Payne Foundation
49. Considering payment of bill for material published in *The Journal*
50. Discussing a publication of the National Association for Reduction of Taxes
51. Authorizing life membership key

BOARD OF TRUSTEES

The duties of the Board of Trustees, as enumerated in the Act of Incorporation (Section 7), are: the "safekeeping and investment" of the permanent fund, "and of all other funds which the corporation may receive by donation, bequest or devise"; issuing "orders on the treasurer for the payment of all bills approved by the Board of

Directors, or by the president and secretary of the association acting under authority of the Board of Directors"; electing the secretary of the association and fixing "the compensation and the term of his office for a period not to exceed four years."

The by-laws add the duty of making a full report of the finances of the association to the Executive Committee annually.

The minutes of the meetings of this board have not been published regularly. Such records as are available, however, record the following activities:

1. Receiving report of auditors
2. Voting to secure legal opinion as to powers and duties of Board of Trustees, Board of Directors, and Executive Committee
3. Making decisions in various matters involving the funds of the association, rentals, deposits, etc.
4. Asking advice of Board of Directors as to purchase of property
5. Arranging for bonding of members of headquarters staff
6. Establishing, by formal resolution, a Fund for Homes for Retired Teachers
7. Fixing salary of secretary of association
8. Transferring income from permanent fund to current fund
9. Discussing heating and other matters at headquarters building
10. Discussing need for more space for headquarters staff and various ways of providing it
11. Authorizing chairman to handle permanent investments

It should be noted that the president of the association is a member of the Executive Committee and of the Board of Trustees; that the chairman of the Board of Trustees is a member of the Executive Committee; that it has become a common practice for members of the Board of Trustees, other than the chairman, to attend the meetings of the Executive Committee and to participate in the discussions although they are not allowed to vote; and that Executive Committee members are welcome to attend meetings of the Board of Trustees if they wish to do so.

Of the various leadership subgroups established under the constitution and by-laws, the Board of Trustees is the only one having specifically defined functions. The latter body performs acts of both legislative and executive kinds, but within a limited field, namely, acts related to the relatively permanent economic possessions of the group.[2] The only activity which does not fall clearly

[2] Cf. Professor Ross's dictum that ". . . diversified property interests requiring intelligent care if they are to remain productive press home upon a membership the wisdom of entrusting their management to a select few."—*Op. cit.*, p. 276.

Activities and Objectives

under this category is that involved in the election of the secretary of the association.

There are three kinds of activities in which the Representative Assembly alone engages: (1) It determines changes in the fundamental structure of the association, that is, it amends the by-laws; (2) it acts as a final receiving body, a body to which all other subgroups make reports, but it does not itself make reports to any other subgroup; and (3) it exchanges formal greetings with other groups on behalf of the association as a whole.[3] Beyond these three kinds of activities, the Representative Assembly's functions are of the same kinds as those performed by the Board of Directors and by the Executive Committee. Action is not taken in so many specific cases by the assembly as by the other bodies, however, the difference no doubt being adequately accounted for by the fact that it meets only once a year whereas the others meet two or more times, and by the further fact that its size creates a situation which is tacitly accepted as precluding the consideration of many matters which may be more expeditiously disposed of in the smaller bodies. Its willingness to delegate authority to the smaller subgroups in so many matters may be due to the fact that the ordinary member of the assembly does not have much at stake in the outcome.[4]

The Board of Directors engages in deliberative and legislative activities of great variety. There is no explicit prohibition upon its assumption of executive functions, and some of its activities are more or less executive in character, such, for example, as the creation of a committee which has been authorized by the Representative Assembly. However, the factors of size and geographic distribution of its membership and consequent infrequency of meeting make it impractical for this body to assume any considerable share of the strictly executive functions of the association.

Because the Executive Committee meets oftener; because it is smaller [5] than the Representative Assembly and Board of Directors; because it is made up of persons familiar with the work of the association; because members of the Board of Trustees and of the Headquarters Staff are always on hand for consultation; because it deals with many specific and detailed matters of an executive kind,

---

[3] There would be less meaning in these formal greetings, probably a less favorable reaction to them, if they were issued by a smaller subgroup. Cf. discussion of large committees, pp. 53-54.
[4] Ross, E. A., *Principles of Sociology*, p. 275.
[5] It consists of five members.

general authority for which has been delegated to it—for these reasons, the Executive Committee's record includes a greater *number* of specific acts than does the record of the assembly or the Board of Directors. It acts formally upon such specific matters as the details of assignment of rooms in the headquarters building and the use of cheaper paper in *The Journal*. It also acts occasionally in matters which may easily involve the association in far-reaching policies, as when it asks for a place for a member of the association on the convention program of the American Federation of Labor. This committee also exercises a judicial or interpretative function, as, for example, when it passes upon the "legality" of the election of state directors, and when it accepts the constitution and by-laws of a new department.

Natural products of ill-defined authority are overlapping of function and duplication of activity. However, if the authority of each of these bodies were sharply defined and limited, it is probable that the resulting inflexibility would cause the machinery to be much more cumbersome than it is and that there would be serious delays. Under the present arrangement, there is a centralized executive staff [6] of paid specialists for executing the general and specific directions of the association and performing such functions as have been routinized. There is a small, somewhat experienced Executive Committee, whose members are available for the consideration of current issues and the making of decisions that have to be made immediately in matters that are not of a sufficiently routine character to be entrusted to the employed executive officers. This committee has, or assumes, authority in all important phases of activity except the changing of the by-laws and the control of the permanent funds and property of the association. In the latter field, the Board of Trustees has full responsibility, and its members are so few in number that it is feasible for them to meet frequently, either separately or with the Executive Committee. Thus it is possible to secure action on most of the unforeseen, urgent issues arising during the intervals between the sessions of the larger bodies. Matters that are not urgent can await the meeting of the more adequately representative Board of Directors for their first consideration or for the presentation of a recommended course of action upon them on the part of the smaller subgroups, and such action as has been taken on urgent matters can be reviewed. The source of authority for all

[6] Chap. VI of the present study.

Activities and Objectives

these bodies is the Representative Assembly and it properly exercises the function of receiving reports as a safeguard against a misuse of delegated authority and against the over-concentration of power in the hands of a few.[7]

The assumption is that only as a result of a complete listing of the kinds of activity carried on can a group be understood. This chapter and the two chapters preceding it have been devoted to this end. The picture presented is one of a complex behavior pattern— a pattern made complex by the great number of activities; the difference in the importance and in the technical character of activities; the difference in size and authority of subgroups engaged in group activities; the fact that some functions are performed by paid and some by unpaid persons; the fact that some activities deal with internal functionings and some with external relationships; the geographic factors of time and distance.

In the three succeeding chapters, activities which have to do with group conflict, coöperation, and control will be isolated from this complex pattern and subjected to analysis and interpretation.

[7] The assembly as at present constituted may not be an effective check upon concentration of power, however, because it may itself be dominated by a few leaders. Various aspects of this situation are discussed in Chaps. III and IV of the present study.

CHAPTER VIII

CONFLICT AS AN ELEMENT IN THE ACTIVITY OF THE ASSOCIATION

That every group situation has in it the possibility of conflict is so universally observed as to need no proof. In certain matters a member of any group may find his personal interest opposed to that of some other member, his self-advantage in conflict with group policy. The special interest of a particular group may interfere with that of other groups.[1] Because there is the possibility that internal conflict may disrupt the group and that external opposition may weaken it, groups and their leaders have reason to be concerned about conflicting attitudes and activities. Still, under certain conditions, the values of conflict are positive rather than negative. "Conflict has sociological interest," observes Simmel, "inasmuch as it either produces or modifies communities of interest, unifications, organizations. . . ."[2] And, according to Park and Burgess: "Conflict is an organizing principle in society. Just as the individual, under the influence of contact and conflict with other individuals, acquires a status and develops a personality, so groups of individuals, in conflict with other groups, achieve unity, organization, group consciousness. . . ."[3]

The relationships in which potential conflict inheres within and without the association, appear to be the following:

1. Between individual members of the association
2. Between a minority of one or more and a majority of the members
3. Between special-interest subgroups (departments, for example)
4. Between special-function subgroups (executive divisions and committees, for example)
5. Between the sexes
6. Between subgroups and the association as a whole (a department and the association, for example)
7. Between the group as a whole and other groups

---
[1] Ross, E. A., *Principles of Sociology*, pp. 158-59.
[2] Simmel, G., "The Sociology of Conflict" (Translated from the German by Albion W. Small), *American Journal of Sociology*, IX (1903-1904), p. 490.
[3] Park R. E. and Burgess, E. W., *Introduction to the Science of Sociology*, p. 642.

Conflict as an Element in Activity

INTERNAL CONFLICT

It is not difficult to find evidences of conflict among the members. There has been occasional difference of opinion as to policy, as shown in the official records and in press comments. There was for a time opposition to the ex officio representation of the state superintendents of education in the Representative Assembly.[4] But this seems to have spent its force, probably because these ex officio members have not assumed the active leadership which was feared by some members. The mere voicing of the opposition may have prevented the anticipated results. A proposed change in the basis of representation in the assembly met with stiff opposition at the 1928 convention.[5] There is reason for believing that there is some difference of opinion in the association about the continuation of the policy of permitting each retiring president become a life director.[6]

Occasionally there is evidence of difference of opinion within the association on such an important matter of policy as support of the bill for the creation of a national Department of Education. Usually, however, resolutions in support of this measure have been adopted unanimously, and never with more than a trifling negative vote. There is no evidence of bitter feeling as a result of these conflicts, no sharpness, no personal animosity. The association does express itself sharply, however, or does assent to the sharp comment of its leaders, against its own members who attack its policies or principles in a public manner. Although its general practice is not to mention names in its reports and resolutions, it has gone so far as to attack a life director (past president) by name because of his public statement concerning the responsibility of the schools for lawlessness, and to belittle his "life record" on the ground of "lack of knowledge or appreciation of the common schools of the nation."[7] This past president and another prominent person in the field of education (also referred to by name), who had attacked the mounting cost of education, were characterized in the address of the president of the association as "Educational plutocrats," "modern Mediævalists," "educational reactionaries." It seemed to be especially

---
[4] "The Reorganized National Education Association," *School Review*, XXVIII (Sept., 1920), pp. 481-86; Minutes of Representative Assembly, *Add. and Proc.*, 1923, p. 48.
[5] *Add. and Proc.*, 1928, pp. 1067-75.
[6] Minutes of Board of Directors meeting, *Add. and Proc.*, 1928, p. 1082.
[7] Secretary's Report, *Add. and Proc.*, 1924, p. 103.

resented that these attacks should come from "foes within our own household."[8]

One conflict which became quite well defined early in the period being studied was that between the association as a whole, or its leaders, and the Department of Superintendence. Withdrawal of the department as a separate organization is hinted at as a possibility in the records and was undoubtedly in the minds of many.[9] A break was avoided in this instance by giving this department, the most powerful of all the subgroups, more autonomy, and it now coöperates fully with the parent organization, its coöperation being "based on good feeling."[10]

Recognizing the possibility of internal conflicts inherent in certain situations and relationships, the association has made adjustments to prevent the materialization of these conflicts. This is true in the matter of its own relationships to the departments, these being given more autonomy in recent years than they formerly possessed. Another illustration of this policy is the "gentlemen's agreement" to alternate the presidency of the association between the sexes.[11] The fact that women hold more of the other offices than formerly, as shown elsewhere in the present study,[12] is probably to be considered as evidence of this general recognition of potential conflict, although there is no record of any agreement concerning sex representation except as to the presidency. The conflict between the sexes over control of the offices had reached considerable proportions at the time of Alexander's study[13] and later,[14] but it is now of such minor proportions as to be indiscernible. Potential sectional conflict over the choice of place for holding the annual convention is avoided

---

[8] Jones, Olive M., "The Nation's Teachers," *Add. and Proc.*, 1924, pp. 184-85; also *School and Society*, XX (July 5, 1924), pp. 1-9.

Cf. Simmel, G., *op. cit.*, pp. 519-20. Reference is made to "that hostility, the intensity of which is based upon association and unity which is by no means always likeness. . . . Here, instead of the consciousness of difference, an entirely new motive emerges—the peculiar phenomenon of social hatred, that is, of hatred toward a member of the group, not from personal motives, but because he threatens the existence of the group. In so far as such a danger threatens through feud within the group, the one party hates the other not alone on the material ground which instigated the quarrel, but also on the sociological ground, namely, that we hate the enemy of the group, as such; that is, the one from whom danger to its unity threatens."

[9] See, for example, the report of the Atlantic City meeting in *School and Society*, XIII (March 19, 1921), pp. 331-37.

[10] Personal communication from chief executive officer.

[11] P. 67 of the present study.

[12] Chap. IV of the present study.

[13] Pp. 173-76 of the present study.

[14] P. 11 of the present study.

Conflict as an Element in Activity 131

by an "understanding" that East, West, Middle West, and South may have it in rotation. The possibility of conflict between departments, or at least between the members engaged in various specialized educational activities, has been minimized by addresses at convention sessions in which the particular points of view of each subgroup were communicated to the other subgroups.[15] Another illustration of an effort to avoid a serious conflict situation within the association is to be found in the adoption by the Executive Committee of the rule prohibiting members of the executive staff from taking part in the contests for the various offices.[16] In line with the same aim is the practice of minimizing differences between majority and minority by such statements as the following:[17]

> There is no fight directed toward the private or religious schools. There should be none. These institutions have their place and receive the encouragement of the association. There are thousands of teachers in private schools in the membership of the association. These schools should have the respect of public-school authorities. Great contributions to human betterment are made by both religious and secular private schools as well as by our great system of public education. Our children and youth need these schools and many more. The big interests work great injury to private schools in attempting to prejudice them against the public schools. The teachers of private schools and all other teachers realize that in a democracy the foundation for success is a democratic education. The public schools are admirably adapted to give that training; the private schools ought to teach in harmony with the same ideas. There is no fight on between these forces themselves. Nine-tenths of our public-school teachers appreciate the mission and importance of our private educational enterprises and nine-tenths of our private-school teachers value and understand the necessity of public-school education. These big interests should not be permitted to drive the wedge which might separate them.

Whether the policy of keeping adverse criticism of the association out of the columns of *The Journal*[18] is adopted because of fear of internal conflict is uncertain. If this is the motive, there is some reason for believing the policy to be ill-advised.

In a way, open opposition preserves society. Without the power and the right to oppose what we believe to be tyranny, obstinacy, caprice, or stupidity, we should terminate our relations with persons who betray such characteristics. Protest affords relief, gives us the feeling that we are not completely crushed in relationships which otherwise we should find unendurable, and from which we should extricate ourselves at any cost. In

---
[15] Pp. 78-79, 83 of the present study.
[16] Secretary's Report, *Add. and Proc.*, 1923, p. 100.
[17] *Add. and Proc.*, 1924, p. 104.
[18] See p. 108 of the present study.

any voluntary association the corking up by the dominant element of the protest and opposition of the rest is likely to lead to the splitting of the group. . . .[19]

Moreover, it is entirely possible that conditions outside the association might affect the amount of overt opposition within the association. For example, it is probable that within the past few years there has been a change in the relationships between superintendents and teachers in the school systems of the country, in the form of a diminution of autocratic authority on the part of the executive officers and an increase in teacher participation in the determination of school policies, with a resulting decrease of opposition between these two classes. Most of the superintendents being men and most of the teachers being women, the result would be an apparent decrease in the sex rivalry within the association, for the former clashes between the factions were probably based fully as much upon differences in educational position as upon sex.[20]

Another element in the situation tending to keep down the amount of internal conflict is a selective process operating to cause certain persons not to become members. This would eliminate those who believe that a teachers' association should be a "fighting" organization, for this association is not known for its aggressiveness in behalf of higher salaries and other matters related to teachers' welfare.[21] If these were members, it seems probable that they would not only tend to involve the group in a greater amount of external conflict, but in an increase of internal conflict as well, because of the relation of conflict procedures to temperament and to aggressive personality types in general.[22] In addition to these, others who find themselves in disagreement with some well-established aim of the association, such, for example, as the creation of a Federal Department of Education, are not likely to become members.[23] Catholic teachers, supporting the position of their church against this measure, are

[19] Ross, E. A., *op. cit.*, p. 162.
Cf. Simmel, G., *op. cit.*, p. 493.
[20] Ortschild, Viola, "Grade Teachers Associations," *Oregon Teachers Monthly*, XXI, pp. 14-19, September, 1916.
Engelhardt, F. W., "Organization of Teachers," *School and Society*, XI, pp. 468-69, April 17, 1920.
[21] Curtis, W. C., "Unionization from the Standpoint of a University Teacher," *Educational Review*, LX (Sept., 1920), p. 92.
[22] Ross, E. A., *op. cit.*, p. 158.
[23] Cf. Giddings, F. H., "Cultural Conflicts and the Organization of Sects," as quoted by Park, R. E. and Burgess, E. W., *Introduction to the Science of Sociology*, pp. 613-14: "It is assumed . . . that any idea or group of ideas, any belief or group of beliefs, may happen to be or may become a common interest, shared by a small or a

not likely to join an association that is openly lobbying for the measure. Again, those serving in a specialized field in education which is not now promoted by the association, tend to organize independently rather than to join an organization in which they would have to compete with other specialized interests for recognition and support.

The extremity of the position which the association has apparently taken with regard to keeping down internal opposition is indicated in the unrefuted statement of a delegate at the 1928 convention to the effect that "the National Education Association in its resolutions has never taken part in any local controversy," that is, any local issue upon which its own members were divided.[24]

EXTERNAL CONFLICT

The association members have a common interest in the welfare of their special class, that is, teachers in general, and especially public school teachers. This interest is rather directly opposed to that of taxpayers, school patrons, school board members, and legislators in some matters, or at least is believed by some of these other classes to be opposed to the "public" interest. This would be true of such matters as increased salaries, indefinite teacher tenure, sabbatical leave, teachers' pensions, legal recognition of professional functions, and federal subsidies for education. The association has taken issue with these natural opponents, including in its conflict activities: passing resolutions, appointing committees and directing executive divisions to study and report, publishing its general points of view and the results of investigations, persuading by means of the press and the lobby—all as detailed elsewhere in this study.

In a few instances the association has taken issue with a particular group over a particular occurrence. When an organization of convention exhibitors found fault with certain regulations controlling commercial exhibits, the Executive Committee adopted a statement asserting in positive terms the right of the association to determine all rules and regulations in cases of this kind.[25] On one occasion the

---

large number of individuals. It may draw and hold them together in bonds of acquaintance, of association, even of coöperation. It thus may play a group-making rôle. Contradictory ideas or beliefs, therefore, may play a group-making rôle in a double sense. Each draws into association the individual minds that entertain it or find it attractive. Each also repels those minds to whom it is repugnant, and drives them toward the group which is being formed about the contradictory idea or belief. . . ."

[24] *Add. and Proc.*, 1928, p. 1077.
[25] "Minutes of Executive Committee," *Add. and Proc.*, 1926, p. 1094.

Executive Committee telegraphed to a city superintendent and a president of a school board protesting against the ruling which prevented certain principals from attending the convention.[26] Several times the association through its resolutions or by means of a statement of one of its leaders has taken a stand in support of one of its prominent members who was under attack. In one case, for instance, the president of the association wrote to the secretary of a state association, evidently with the intention that the latter would use the communication in the fight which was being waged, in part as follows:

> The National Education Association cannot sit by and see one of its honored members ... made the victim of political intrigue. ... I officially protest against the summary and unwarranted action of [the] Governor['s] ... personally selected trustees, and hereby offer our services to ... all ... organizations ... which are working to save that state and the nation from an educational calamity and to return Dr. S—— to the presidency of the university. Let me know in what way we can act most effectively.[27]

Attacks made by individuals or by small or little known organizations upon the association or upon any of the policies for which it stands may be met by silence, as the following quotation from the minutes of the Executive Committee will show: [28]

> The committee discussed the question as to whether the association should give formal attention to the pamphlet, "Sanctified Squander," a pamphlet published by the National Association for the Reduction of Taxes, Cleveland, Ohio. It was finally decided not to present the question before the Representative Assembly at the present time fearing that such action would attach undue importance to an insignificant pamphlet.

The secretary of the association did refer to it in his annual report, however, and sought to discredit it. Later, too, *The Journal* printed the reply that a prominent member of the association made to the pamphlet.[29]

However, even the attacks of individuals of no great prestige may bring forth sharp official rejoinders, as for instance, in the annual address of one of the presidents:[30]

> [There] is a man on our western coast who has recently added a book on public education to his muck-raking series of publications. In it he bit-

---

[26] "Minutes of Executive Committee," *Add. and Proc.*, 1926, pp. 1093-94.
[27] "Association Urges Suzzallo's Return," *Journal of the National Education Association*, XV (Dec., 1926), p. 268; additional cases are referred to in *Add. and Proc.*, 1925, pp. 1003-4; p. 998; 1926, p. 1085; 1923, p. 55; 1924, p. 56.
[28] *Add. and Proc.*, 1928, pp. 1100-1.
[29] *Journal of National Education Association*, XVII (Nov., 1928), pp. 233-34.
[30] Jones, Olive M., *op. cit.*

Conflict as an Element in Activity

terly attacks school people and the National Education Association. . . .
Misrepresentation of motives, half truths, hearsay, and scandal are the instruments used to turn the gullible against the National Education Association and give the foes of national, democratic education a chance to rush into the breach thus made. There is internal evidence that many of his statements are founded upon unproven assertions of foes within our household. Defeated in their attempts at creating schism in the association, they avail themselves of his ready ear to secure publicity for charges already overwhelmingly refuted.

[The statements are] . . . false and libelous. . . .

No estates in California, no salaries as paid agitators, no incomes from bulletins and surveys are our reward. . . .

Another case, somewhat similar, but involving an influential organization, is recorded in the secretary's report for 1928.[31] To chapters of the Daughters of the American Revolution, pamphlets had been distributed listing the National Education Association, along with other groups, as being sympathetic with communistic ideals, and including a former president of the association on a "black list" of men of questionable patriotic loyalty. Since it appeared that the pamphlet "represented the views of that great patriotic organization," the secretary wrote to its president protesting that the members of the association were loyal, and branding the statements in the pamphlet as false. Having received a reply to the effect that the head of the other organization had "always held the National Education Association in high esteem," the secretary reported to the association at its annual convention that "the incident closes with a continuance of the spirit of coöperation and goodwill which has characterized the relationship between our organizations for many years."

The effort to secure the creation by Congress of a national Department of Education, which has been reported as the principal activity of the Division of Legislative Service (Chapter VI) has brought the association into conflict with various organizations. It has carried on this conflict by (1) securing the support of influential persons and groups, having them endorse the measure by letters and formal resolutions and by appearance at congressional hearings; (2) presenting arguments and counter arguments to individual congressmen and at public hearings; (3) giving publicity to the names and membership of the specific organizations supporting the measure, but not to the names and numbers of its opponents, they being

[31] *Add. and Proc.*, 1928, pp. 1147-48.

vaguely referred to as "private and church schools," "opponents," "selfish opposition," "enemies of public education";[32] (4) giving publicity through *The Journal* and in special publications to the arguments in support of the creation of the department but omitting negative arguments;[33] and (5) keeping the members' ranks solidly united by direct appeals to the members from the leaders,[34] as in the following: "There never has been a time in the history of the association when unity of purpose and solidarity of ranks were so much needed as at the present moment."[35]

There is abundant evidence that the association, or at least the leadership that it has had for these eleven years, has been vitally interested in fighting for the Department of Education measure. In one instance, stung by what it considered a grossly unfair statement concerning the bill in a newspaper in the city where the annual convention was being held, and taunted by the mayor's welcoming representatives with the statement that that city wanted no interference in educational matters from the United States or anybody else, the association proceeded to pile up evidence not only of its formal, but of its enthusiastic, support of the proposal. "The challenge . . . was taken up by nearly every speaker on the general programs of the convention." The report of the Legislative Commission's activities in behalf of the measure "brought the delegates to their feet." The motion that the commission's report "be printed and widely

[32] The Chamber of Commerce of the United States was referred to by name after its referendum to its membership had placed it on record as opposed to the bill. The Catholic Church and its various organizations seem never to be referred to specifically, even though they are apparently the most active opponents of the measure. For instance, the official record of a public hearing on the "Education Bill" in 1926 (Joint Hearings before the Committee on Education and Labor, United States Senate, and the Committee on Education, House of Representatives, 69th Congress, First Session, on Senate 291 and House of Representatives 5000 and Senate 2841, pp. 297-311, Feb. 24, 25, 26, 1926. U. S. Government Printing Office, Washington, 1926) gives a list of 575 organizations, almost all of them Catholic, as opponents of the bill, as compared to 43 proponents, those organizations that had endorsed the bill by petition. Why the association should fail to mention this well-organized opposition specifically is not clear. It may be due to the general American hesitancy to introduce religious elements into non-religious controversies, or it may be due to the more practical point of view that it is not good policy to alienate actual and prospective association members who happen to be Catholics.

[33] *Journal of National Education Association*, XVI (May, 1927), p. 161.

[34] Cf. Vincent, G. E., "The Rivalry of Social Groups," *American Journal of Sociology*, XVI, (1910-1911), p. 474: "Struggle forces upon the group the necessity of cozening, beguiling, managing its members."

[35] Report of Legislative Division, *Add. and Proc.*, 1925, p. 1051.

Cf. the stimulation of morale as reported by E. S. Bogardus, *Fundamentals of Social Psychology*, p. 334: "Morale is often developed by a studied appeal to the spirit of soldiership whether individuals are working or fighting. They are asked to be good soldiers, to obey unquestioningly, to endure until the end, to fight a good fight. . . ."

circulated throughout the United States" was carried with only two dissenting votes out of more than 800.[36]

The association engages in definite conflict activities upon issues that are imminent and specific and also upon those that are of a long-time, general character. Examples of the latter would be salary, retirement and tenure standards, and national recognition of education.[37] The association has made the carrying on of its major conflicts a more or less specialized function through the creation of commissions and committees and headquarters divisions. Certainly the Legislative Division should be considered a conflict agency, and some of the activities of the Division of Research and the Division of Publications are clearly in the nature of indirect, if not of direct, conflict, in that they furnish materials to be used by the specialized conflict agencies and by the membership.

Examples of conflict activities in connection with imminent, specific issues are the communications and resolutions protesting against the removal of school officials from their positions. In such cases, no special machinery is set up for performing the function. The activities involved are incidental to leadership. In the nature of the cases nothing can be done except to voice protests, and these have at least as much force if they come from the official leaders or leadership subgroups such as the Executive Committee or the Representative Assembly as they would have if a special agency were to be set up for the purpose, and it is possible that they carry even more weight. In any case, the activity is usually of short

[36] Ryan, W. Carson, Jr., "The National Education Association at Boston," *School and Society*, XVI (July 15, 1922), pp. 57-64.

[37] The association's activities in behalf of the creation of a Department of Education have sometimes placed it more or less in a position of apparent opposition to the United States Bureau of Education (now called "Office of Education"), in that the need for a change would necessarily require proof that the present governmental agency is not functioning satisfactorily. For example, an official representative of the association stated at a public hearing: ". . . the Bureau of Education has failed in the collection of reliable, complete, and current statistical information on the level that we would expect if we had had a department of education. . . ." But he prefaced this adverse criticism with such comments as these: "The Bureau of Education has fully capitalized such resources as it has had." . . . "I have nothing but praise for it as an organization." ". . . The Bureau of Education has done fully as well as could reasonably be expected. . . ." (Hearing before the Committee on Education, House of Representatives, 70th Congress, First Session, on H. R. 7.—U. S. Government Printing Office, Washington, 1928.) This is not clearly an expression of a conflict attitude, although the complimentary comments may indicate that the speaker was aware of an undercurrent of conflict between his organization and the Bureau.

Certainly the official position of the association, as found in the records, has not been one of opposition to the Bureau of Education, but of opposition to a system which furnishes what the association considers inadequate national support for education.

duration, commonly limited to the formulation and publication of one message or resolution, so that no special agency seems necessary.

The association certainly cannot be called a militant or "fighting" group. The tone of its conflict pronouncements is mild and conciliatory, in the main, the only exception being its response to attacks upon itself or its prominent members, in which instance it does express itself sharply or at least decisively. Even in these latter cases, it is apparently concerned to close the incidents of conflict in a "spirit of coöperation and good will." The aim apparently is to keep a present feeling of opposition on the part of another organization from being perpetuated or intensified, so far as this is possible. The conciliatory effort is properly to be interpreted as a conflict procedure.[38] The association needs the good will, passive if not active, of all groups that are not its natural enemies, if it is to carry on an effective attack upon its natural opponents. Whether the relatively nonaggressive, conciliatory procedure is too large an element in the conflict activities of the group can be only a matter of opinion. Certainly only the unthinking or temperamentally contentious would ban its use or belittle its importance.

There is no measure of the effectiveness of the association's conflict activities. Probably they helped to promote the growth of the organization during the early years of this period.[39] Presumably they are somewhat effective in the direction intended, their value depending upon such factors as timeliness, relation to the conflict effort of other groups, prestige of the association and of its leaders. Certainly their effectiveness is not due to the numerical strength of the association. Through their total voting power the members could scarcely hope to elect more than four or five members of Congress, even if the whole membership were concentrated in that number of congressional districts. And since teachers tend to be distributed rather uniformly throughout the population, their actual strength in any political contest, national, state, or local, is negligible. In order to be effective in direct attack through political channels, they must necessarily secure the active coöperation of many nonmembers, even of many who are not engaged in education. This they are doing with some success, as will be shown in the succeeding chapter.

[38] Cf. C. H. Cooley's discussion of nonresistance as a conflict procedure, *Human Nature and the Social Order*, pp. 276-79.
[39] Pp. 25-28 of the present study.

CHAPTER IX

THE VARIETIES AND FORMS OF GROUP COÖPERATION

In a sense, the very existence of a group is evidence of the fact of the coöperation of its members. In the present instance, the willing or unwilling payment of the annual membership fee of two dollars is an act of coöperation with other persons in the carrying on of an enterprise for which money is needed. If the act of joining is wholly voluntary, the payment of the fee would indicate an attitude of coöperation. If there is an element of compulsion behind the act,[1] it would still be an instance of coöperation, even though involuntary.[2]

The existence of any degree of division of labor within any group is prima facie evidence of coöperation.[3] In the National Education Association, as already pointed out, there is a complex specialization of function, with departments and divisions and committees and other subgroups all performing their parts in the common enterprise.

The fact that this association, in spite of its very general character, has attracted a large number of persons into its membership points to the conclusion that American teachers, in addition to their specialized educational interests, are conscious of having common objectives and that they desire to coöperate in the attainment of those ends that they hold in common. Although not a federation in form, the association provides an opportunity in its departments for carrying out the distinct purposes of the various occupational subgroups, purposes in which other subgroups could not be expected to coöperate actively; whereas, independently of department membership, certain activities in which all teachers have an interest are coördinated under a "single, comprehensive, intelligent plan," thus avoiding much duplication of effort.[4]

In addition to its coördination of the coöperative efforts of its specialized membership, the association, through its Representative

---
[1] Pp. 22-23 of the present study.
[2] Ross, E. A., *Principles of Sociology*, p. 246.
[3] Park, R. E. and Burgess, E. W., *Introduction to the Science of Sociology*, pp. 714-18.
[4] Ross, E. A., *op. cit.*, pp. 257-58.

Assembly, constitutes a machinery for coöperation in the formulation and expression of the opinions of the members, the "will of the people." Certain defects in the machinery have been pointed out.[5] Still the fact remains that the procedure is one under which all members, in theory at least, coöperate indirectly in such matters as establishing standards and initiating activities.

Another general coöperative function is involved in what Ross would call the "organization of thought." [6] Addresses are delivered, discussion is carried on, the "thinking of many men" on educational matters is pooled. Because this is a continuing organization, keeping permanent records of its thinking and discussion, its coöperation in thought organization extends back into the past and forward into the future.

In addition to the coöperation involving members and subgroups within an organization, it is important to discover the coöperative relationships into which the group as a whole enters. Does this association take the initiative in establishing such relationships with other groups, or is it inert until approached? Does it coöperate only in specific enterprises, or does it enter into general coöperative agreements? What is the nature of its coöperative activities? What are the motives for its coöperative activities? Does it have a policy of coöperation, or are its activities in this direction fortuitous and opportunistic?

The association has sought the coöperation of a large number of organizations in its efforts to secure the establishment of a Federal Department of Education. Those that have responded favorably, at least to the extent of adopting a resolution favoring the proposal, include the following:[7]

>National Committee for a Department of Education
>American Federation of Teachers
>American Federation of Labor
>National Council of Women [8]
>National Congress of Parents and Teachers
>General Federation of Women's Clubs
>National League of Women Voters [9]
>Supreme Council, Scottish Rite of Freemasonry, Southern Jurisdiction, United States

[5] Chap. III of the present study.
[6] Ross, E. A., *op. cit.*, pp. 283-84.
[7] "Report of the Legislative Division," *Add. and Proc.*, 1926, pp. 1139-40; *Annual Report of the Secretary* (pamphlet) 1928, p. 43.
[8] Thirty national organizations.
[9] Organizations in 44 states.

International Council of Religious Education [10]
National Council of Jewish Women
National Women's Christian Temperance Union
American Association of University Women
National Federation of Business and Professional Women's Clubs
General Grand Chapter, Order of the Eastern Star
National Board Young Women's Christian Association
National Women's Trade Union League
National Society, Daughters of the American Revolution
National Federation of Music Clubs
American Library Association
American Vocational Association
Women's Relief Corps
Federal Council of Churches of Christ in America [11]
National Kindergarten Association
American Home Economics Association
American Hellenic Educational Progressive Association
American Nurses' Association
Junior Order of American Mechanics
Woman's Missionary Council of the Methodist Episcopal Church, South
Osteopathic Women's National Association

It is apparent that the association has little in common with many of the organizations listed. It has asked and received their support, not of all its policies, but of one only, and it in turn would certainly not be willing to support all the principles and policies favored by all these groups.

In addition to these organizations which have coöperated in regard to this specific matter, for the most part after being invited to do so by the association, there are numerous others that have expressed their willingness to coöperate in general terms. The secretary of the association reported to the Representative Assembly in 1927:[12] "The American Medical Association, the American Bar Association, and the National Editorial Association are among those most interested in our work. We have had letters from each of these and others, expressing interest in the big program of this association. They want us to call upon them for help. . . ." He quoted from a telegram received from the National Editorial Association: ". . . Both these great educational organizations are working along similar lines for the general good. We have much in common, looking to the future welfare of our country. . . ." The

---
[10] Thirty-six Protestant organizations.
[11] Thirty Protestant denominations.
[12] *Add. and Proc.*, 1927, p. 1086.

letters and the telegram may of course be merely expressions of goodwill, from one executive to another, but they would seem to show a general coöperative attitude.

Coöperation with the American Legion is more definitely indicated in the record, although here, too, it seems to be described in rather general terms. The resolutions of the 1921 Representative Assembly refer to the relationship as follows: [13]

> We gratefully acknowledge the coöperation of other great national organizations in the development and promotion of an American program of education.
>
> We are glad to coöperate with the American Legion in the establishment of a universal requirement of English as the only basic language of instruction in all schools—public, private, and parochial—and we commend heartily their demand that thoroughgoing instruction in American history and civics be required of all students for graduation from elementary and from secondary schools. We welcome their coöperation in the establishment of a longer school year, and in the enforcement throughout the United States of compulsory education to the end of the high school period.

It was reported the next year that the agreement between the association and the committee on education of the American Legion "placed the American Legion squarely behind a few essential educational policies and pledged the fullest coöperation of both organizations in the promotion of the interests of the public schools." [14]

There are evidences that the relationship of the association to the American Federation of Labor is quite cordial. At one time the Executive Committee instructed the secretary of the association "to write a letter to Mr. Gompers expressing a desire for a member of the association to have a place on the next program of the American Federation of Labor." [15]

The association rather readily responds with resolutions of endorsement for organizations and measures related in general spirit and aim to any of the activities of the association itself,[16] such as the Junior Red Cross, the National Congress of Parents and Teachers, the National Conference on Outdoor Recreation.

In some cases, coöperation between the association and another organization is furthered by the creation of a joint committee of the two groups, both sharing in the work and in the cost of the enterprise undertaken. There have been from time to time: a Committee

---

[13] *Add. and Proc.*, 1921, p. 27.
[14] Report of the Secretary, *Add. and Proc.*, 1922, pp. 98-99.
[15] *Add. and Proc.*, 1924, p. 87.
[16] See analysis of resolutions in Chap. V of the present study.

to Coöperate with the American School Citizenship League; a Committee to Coöperate with the Children's Bureau; a Committee to Coöperate with the Federation of Women's Clubs; a Committee to Coöperate with the Conference on Limitation of Armaments; a Joint Committee (with the American Medical Association) on Health Problems in Education; a Joint Committee (with the American Library Association) on School Libraries; a Joint Committee (with the American Association of Museums) on School and Museum Relations; a Committee to Coöperate with the National Association of Teachers in Colored Schools; a Committee on Behavior Problems of Children (coöperating with the National Conference of Social Work); a Committee on Coöperation with the World Federation of Education Associations; a Committee on Coöperation with the Bureau of Education; a Committee to Coöperate with the Motion Picture Producers.

In a sense, the local and state associations, even though they are "affiliated" with the national association, are to be considered "outside" organizations. They are organized independently, they determine their own fees and programs of work, they may discontinue their formal "affiliation" at any time.[17] That the relationship is one with considerable vitality in it, and that the leaders of the state associations have a genuine interest in promoting the welfare of the larger body is shown by Granrud's study [18] in which it is reported that forty-six officers of state teachers associations ranked "National Education Association membership, organization, etc.," fifth in importance in a list of fifty-four educational problems.

It has not been, up to the present, the policy of the national body to give active aid to the state associations in their internal problems, such as organization and membership, or in their attack upon educational problems which are confined within their own state boundaries, such as the effort to secure the enactment of state educational legislation.

On one occasion, however, the secretaries of the state associations were invited to meet with the officers of the national association for the purpose of planning a coöperative attack on legislative problems, and eighteen of the state secretaries attended the conference. "The object of the conference, as stated by . . . [the president of the Na-

---

[17] The number of affiliated state and local associations listed in the Official Manual for Delegates in 1928 was 787.
[18] Granrud, John, *The Organization and Objectives of State Teachers Associations,* pp. 64-65.

tional Education Association] was to secure, first, the coöperation of the state associations with the National Education Association on Federal legislation and Federal policies; second, the coöperation of the National Education Association with the state associations in securing state legislation. The conference discussed at length the present status of the education bill which provides for a Secretary of Education in the President's cabinet. . . . The need of Federal legislation to clear the titles of western states to their school lands was presented. . . . Active measures were authorized in support of this legislation. Conferences were held with . . . [congressmen.]" [19]

In a few cases in which local or state educational leaders have been attacked, the officials of the national association have taken action to support the ones attacked.[20] This can hardly be considered coöperation with state associations, however, for the cases seem to have attracted sufficient public notice and to be of such a character that in reality they are of much more than state-wide significance. The action has been primarily for the purpose of aiding a prominent member of the national association, not of aiding or supporting a state association.

The association is a constituent member of two organizations: the World Federation of Education Associations and the American Council on Education. Its membership is evidence of general formal coöperation with these bodies, the aims and activities of which are, for the former: "To secure international coöperation in educational enterprises; to foster the dissemination of information concerning the progress of education in all its forms among nations and peoples; to cultivate international goodwill; and to promote the interests of peace throughout the world"; [21] and for the latter: "To promote and carry out coöperative action in matters of common interest to associations and institutions interested in university and college education, in patriotic service, and in international educational relations." [22]

The association has realized the need of establishing a general policy with regard to its coöperative relationships. One of the presidents commented in her annual address: [23]

[19] Shankland, S. D., "State Secretaries Meet," *Educational Review*, LXXIII (Feb., 1927), pp. 77-78.
[20] See discussion of external conflict (Chap. VIII).
[21] *A Handbook of Educational Associations and Foundations in the United States*. U. S. Bureau of Education *Bulletin*, 1926, No. 16, p. 82.
[22] *Ibid.*, p. 8.
[23] Jones, Olive M., "The Nation's Teachers," *School and Society*, XX, pp. 6-7.

... It is especially dangerous for teachers' associations to ally themselves too closely with any organization other than one whose devotion to the cause of education of the kind already defined and whose protection of American democratic ideals are assured beyond doubt. Many an organization has a high-sounding name, and a platform talking loudly of democracy and education, whose inside counsels and financial support would prove them inimical to America, chaotic in their consequences if successful, or else autocratic and reactionary in their dictation of educational practice.

Whatever organization we ally ourselves with must give conclusive proof that its aims will aid in the accomplishment of our goal. Whatever alliances we effect should be for a stated time only, and for the accomplishment of a single project, unless this conclusive proof is given.

A year later the Committee on Relationships made the following recommendations, and the Representative Assembly adopted them: [24]

1. ... that the National Education Association establish a policy of defining a time limit for the existence of mutual relationships with allied organizations, requiring reaffirmation or termination at the end of such time limit.[25]

2. ... that the National Education Association shall require all allied organizations to submit to its Executive Committee for approval all policy-making resolutions before using the name of the National Education Association in support of such measures.

3. ... that the secretary of the National Education Association shall notify the heads of departments, committees, sections, or other divisions of the National Education Association, that the name of the National Education Association may not be used in endorsement, or in opposition to any person, policy, resolution, or publication without the consent of the Executive Committee of the National Education Association.

It is quite clear that the association has established a variety of coöperative relationships with a great variety of organizations. In most instances the coöperation does not seem to be very active or vital. It is sometimes limited to a formal expression of a spirit of coöperation or goodwill on the part of another organization at the request of the National Education Association, or vice versa. Even in cases where a joint committee of the two organizations is appointed, or a joint conference of leaders is arranged, or a constituent membership in an organization of wider scope is accepted, or funds are appropriated, the coöperation may be purely formal. It may be the product of a hesitancy to risk giving offense to another organization through refusing or neglecting approval of its requests. Further, when the association asks the coöperation of another group, it may

[24] *Add. and Proc.,* 1925, pp. 184, 984.
[25] The records do not show that any such time limit has been established.

not anticipate or even desire anything more than merely formal approval of one of its own policies. It may simply wish to borrow the prestige of other groups for a purpose of its own, as, for example, in its activity designed to secure the establishment of a Federal Department of Education.

It is not to be expected, in cases of coöperation between an organization as large as this and other national groups, that there would be any great intensity of interest, on the part of the memberships, in the coöperative enterprise. Contacts of most of the members with their own organizations are largely secondary, remote, impersonal. Contacts with a coöperating organization would be even farther removed. Except possibly in the case of the official leadership and the specially appointed coöperating committees, it seems highly probable that the spirit of the group with regard to the various coöperative relationships is of a rather cold, intellectual quality, not characterized by widespread and intense effort within the membership on behalf of the projects that are sponsored primarily by a coöperating organization.

Moreover, as pointed out elsewhere in this study,[26] the adoption of a resolution of coöperation may indicate even the intellectual assent of only a very small minority of members.

From the fact that the association is besought by other organizations to coöperate in their activities, there arise certain undesirable possibilities. It may, because of a desire to avoid bad feeling, yield formal coöperation in measures in which it is not actually interested but to which it is merely not in opposition. It may, because of the lack of proper consideration of measures which it is asked to support, spend more or less of its energy and resources in promoting standards that are not closely related to its own interests.[27]

Because it places no specific time limits upon its coöperative relationships and does not concern itself to terminate them or to keep them subject to continuous review, it may find itself at a particular time publicly on record as supporting a project or an organization which it would not at that time endorse.

A more systematic procedure with regard to the association's coöperative relationships and activities would seem to be highly desirable from every point of view. Machinery should be set up for very careful advance consideration before coöperation is sought or ac-

---

[26] Pp. 91-92 of the present study.
[27] See pp. 91-92 of the present study.

cepted or granted. Sound social policy would dictate that coöperative activities be limited to the number that can be actively and effectively supported and to the kinds that are consistent with, and that may be economically conducted in coördination with, the major activities of the association.[28] These activities and the relationships upon which they depend might well be subjected to constant and critical review to determine whether they should be continued, modified, or terminated.

[28] See pp. 92-93 of the present study.

CHAPTER X

THE ASSOCIATION'S CONTROL OF ITS MEMBERS

"Group control is a process of regulating personal behavior in the direction of real or supposed group welfare."[1] There is a general tendency for groups to practice this "regulation" in a form and to a degree determined by the character of the groups themselves and by their situation. Primitive and advanced, small and large, autocratic and democratic—all kinds of groups tend to impose control in matters which for them are of primary concern. The degree of control practiced varies all the way from that involved in the mere expression of an expectation that members will attend meetings or pay dues to the level where obligations are imposed upon members under penalty of death. Social control is discussed in sociological literature under a multiplicity of titles with a great range of meaning, titles such as tradition, custom, folkways, mores, taboo, ceremonial, myth, religious and political beliefs, dogmas, creeds, public opinion, law, leadership, suggestion, propaganda, education, codes, prestige.[2]

Control in face-to-face or primary groups [3] and in crowds [4] is relatively simple and easily effective as compared with control in groups where the contacts and relationships among the members are largely secondary in character, that is, impersonal and indirect. It is to be noted that for the great mass of members of the National Education Association, the contacts are largely of this secondary character.

Throughout this study attention has been called occasionally to activities and situations that have the effect of controlling members of the association to some degree. These have included membership campaigns with direct and indirect suggestions of leaders to members

---

[1] Bogardus, E. S., *Fundamentals of Social Psychology*, p. 340.
[2] Cf. Ross, E. A., *Social Control*; also Park, R. E. and Burgess, E. W., *Introduction to the Science of Sociology*, pp. 785-864.
[3] Cooley, C. H., *Social Organization*, Chaps. III and IV.
[4] Cf. Park and Burgess, *op. cit.*, p. 788:
"Control in the crowd, where rapport is once established and every individual is immediately responsive to every other is the most elementary form of control. . . . [There is a] direct and spontaneous response of the individual in the crowd to the crowd's dominant mood or impulse. . . ."

Association's Control of Members 149

that their own memberships be renewed and that they persuade others to join the association; with the setting up of conditions that would promote control through a species of compulsion applied mainly by administrative officers in school systems, and through the growth of rivalry and tradition; and through the utilization of the prestige of well-known persons in positions of educational leadership.[5] The fact that *The Journal,* the medium of intra-group communication, is used for presenting the position of the association on issues, and that opposing points of view are excluded, is of significance as related to group control.[6] The conciliatory statements of leaders, minimizing the differences between factions, are intended to result in a control of real or potential conflict.[7]

Then there are the characteristic convention activities. Even for those who attend the annual conventions the face-to-face influencing is relatively small in amount, for the reason that the association is in session for only a few days out of each year. Not a very great number attend more than one session in the capacity of delegates, as shown in an earlier chapter.[8] It is probable that relatively few non-delegates attend consecutive sessions because of the great geographic distance involved, due to the policy of rotating the convention among the various geographic regions. Most of the members have their contacts with the association through delegates and others who, after returning from conventions, make formal and informal reports to organized and unorganized groups about what was said and done at the conventions and of its influence upon their own thought and action, and through *The Journal,* which carries to all members a report of convention resolutions and addresses as well as other materials from official and unofficial leaders.

The association has no specific principles, no code, to which persons must subscribe and which they must observe in order to become or remain members. The recurring resolutions and some of the addresses at the annual conventions furnish evidence that certain standards are accepted by the leaders and at least assented to by the rank and file of delegates as being proper standards for all members to observe. Five of the resolutions listed in Chapter V are

---

[5] Chap. II of the present study. These activities and situations are of course focused upon all teachers, not upon members only. This is true of most of the specific and incidental controls practiced by the association.

[6] P. 108 of the present study.

[7] Pp. 130-31 of the present study.

[8] Chap. IV of the present study.

somewhat specific formulations of behavior patterns for members, namely, those implying the obligations (1) to be loyal to American institutions and ideals, (2) to teach respect and obedience for law, (3) to secure professional training, (4) to join local, state, and national associations of teachers, and (5) to participate in civic affairs. As formulated, these statements apply to all American teachers, not to association members only, and no attempt has been made to determine the extent of their observance.

The addresses classified under the head of "interpretation,"[9] that is, those that define, for the new and uninformed in the group, the practices, points of view, relationships, standards, objectives, which the group has implicitly or explicitly adopted with respect to education, the school, and the association itself, are to be thought of as a means of control of individual members by the group. Some of those classified as "inspiration"—those that assert a connection of the service of the teacher with the maintenance of moretic values such as religious devotion, patriotism, domestic virtue, "character"—are also in the nature of control mechanisms, for they tend to impose serious, conservative points of view. Some of those listed as "stimulation" and as "general and educational philosophy" would likewise be somewhat effective in imposing attitudes.

Even though it lacks precise rules to apply in dealing with its members, an organization of this kind might exercise effective control by dealing with cases of alleged infringement of implicitly accepted behavior norms, as other occupational groups have done, notably the American Association of University Professors and the American Association of Engineers.[10] In one instance the association did proceed to investigate a case which had received a great deal of publicity. This was the "Elgin case." The facts were, briefly, that certain teachers and principals, as part of their fight to remove the superintendent of schools, had taken an active part in a school board election. They were unsuccessful, and some of them were not reelected to their positions. The particular incident which gave the case wide publicity was the suicide of one of the principals.

Acting under instructions from the Representative Assembly, two members of the executive staff proceeded to Elgin to make a firsthand investigation. These investigators made their report to the Executive Committee of the association, which in turn published the

---

[8] Chap. IV of the present study.
[10] Landis, B. Y., *Professional Codes*, p. 98.

Association's Control of Members 151

findings in *The Journal*.[11] The report was mild and conciliatory in tone, declaring that the affair came about as a normal result of existing conditions and a misunderstanding of motives. Still it was somewhat favorable to teachers and principals and opposed to board and superintendent. A concluding paragraph used the incident to support a plank in the association's platform by declaring that "a failure to give proper recognition to the professional status of the teacher will always prove disastrous to the interests of the children, for it tends to drive out of the teaching profession those most worthy to teach. The tendency in all the best school systems is toward a higher respect for the teacher, and more positive assurance of permanency of tenure on the basis of effective service."

This case had in it two of the important relationships covered in established codes of ethics, namely, that of teachers to administrative officers and that of teachers to boards of education.[12] It was anticipated that the association would be asked to make similar investigations in other localities, and it stood ready to do so, but there were no further requests for its services.[13] This probably indicates that this body has not established itself as being capable of dealing with cases adequately. It may imply uncertainty as to the principles which would be used by the association in reaching decisions.

From time to time leaders of the association and others have spoken of the desirability of formulating a code of professional ethics, as numerous state organizations of teachers have done.[14] In 1924 a committee was appointed to study the problems and eventually to draft a code. It has been actively and systematically at work on its task but has not yet (1928) submitted its final report. The association is convinced that a code is needed for the following reasons:[15]

1. The increased power and better training of teachers demand higher standards of professional conduct.
2. Those who have taken up the profession seriously are guided by worthy ethical principles in the main, but need support.

[11] "The Elgin Report," *Journal of the National Education Association*, XI, No. 9 (Nov., 1922), p. 380.
[12] Landis, B. Y., *op. cit.*, pp. 4-9.
[13] "The Secretary's Report." *Add. and Proc.*, 1923, p. 101.
[14] Russell, J. E., "Organization of Teachers," *Educational Review*, LX (Sept., 1920), pp. 129-35; Chambers, George G., "Codes of Ethics for the Teaching Profession," *Annals of the American Academy of Political and Social Science*, CI (May, 1922), pp. 121-27; Lehman, H. C. and Witty, P. A., "Some Suggestions for Making Teaching a Profession," *Educational Review*, LXXIV (Dec., 1927), pp. 258-69; Walsh, M. J., *Teaching as a Profession*, pp. 333-64.
[15] Report of the Committee on Ethics of the Profession, *Add. and Proc.*, 1928, p. 179.

3. The working principles of those who look upon teaching as a profession should be made available to all in order that those who are entering the profession may have as a guide a definition of what a professional teacher is.

4. For the sake of the teacher himself and in the interests of education there should be a formulated code of ethics and means established to give authority to the code.

The committee is proceeding through questionnaire and check-list techniques to get "a cross section of the highest ideals of the members of the profession." From present indications, the code that will be recommended for adoption will consist of a considerable number of specific practices which are to be condemned as unethical. There is nothing in any of the preliminary reports upon which to base a forecast as to what attempt will be made to enforce the provisions of the code.[16]

It is beyond the scope of the present study to determine just how effective the resolutions and addresses are in the thought and action of members, that is, how effective they are as a means of control. They are communicated to the membership through reports of returning delegates, through publication in the annual volumes and in *The Journal* and in other educational periodicals. If they actually reach the members, they certainly have much more than the force of casual suggestion. They are in print; they have been formulated and presented by someone whose name may not be familiar but whose wisdom and worth are demonstrated by the very fact of his active participation in a group that is national in character and relatively large in membership; they have been assented to by convention delegates, who are assumed to be of more than average importance by virtue of their election as delegates. In other words, the factors of remoteness, size, national character, representative form of organization, and printed communication produce a prestige situation likely to cause members' attitudes to tend toward conformity with the principles laid down.

[16] Since this was written, the association has adopted a code which the committee recommended. It is so framed as to apply to all who are engaged in educational work, not merely to members of the association. It consists of general principles which the teacher should apply in his "relations with pupils and to the community," his "relations to the profession," and his "relations to members of the profession." The committee recommended that steps be taken to make the code effective (1) through including it in teacher-training programs, (2) through publishing it in pedagogical magazines and having it discussed at professional gatherings, and (3) through having each state association of teachers create a committee on professional ethics for interpreting and applying the code within its own state.—*Add. and Proc.*, 1929, pp. 179-90.

But these lack precision and completeness as means of control. The statements are general, not specific or detailed, not applicable to particular cases. Formulated as they are by persons only incidentally concerned at the time with permanent standards for the group, and assented to by the delegates without much careful consideration,[17] they would naturally not be precise or complete or even consistent.

One reason why the association is handicapped in any program of code application or enforcement is the fact that it is operating on such a vast scale and is actively seeking members in order to be able to carry on its program. This situation is not in keeping with the setting up of professional standards for admission or with a penalty of expulsion for violation of standards. Not only is the association too inclusive and too heterogeneous, but it is undoubtedly too large and too completely devoid of authority over the loosely "affiliated" subsidiary groups, for attempting to enforce a specific code in all specific cases that might arise under it. Still, because of the prestige which comes from its size and from its national character, it might make a code somewhat effective by carrying on a continuing campaign to acquaint the general public as well as the teaching population with its provisions, thus focusing public as well as professional opinion upon it. Many state and local associations of teachers would be likely to adopt it formally, and some of them would no doubt create machinery for applying its provisions in cases of infraction within their own areas. If a national code of professional ethics were to be vigorously promoted, there is no reason why this organization should not eventually establish a semi-judicial division to which state and local and special associations might refer marginal or doubtful cases involving interpretation of the code.

Another way in which the national association might promote the acceptance and observance of its code would be through inducing teachers colleges and normal schools to present it to their students. A code that is nationally formulated and adopted will have greater prestige with prospective teachers—will be more "impressive"—than one that is framed by a local or state group.

The relatively great mobility of the teaching population makes it highly desirable that there be nation-wide uniformity in the general principles to be included in teachers' codes of ethics. If this association assumes an aggressive policy in the matter, it may extend its

[17] See pp. 91-93 of the present study.

control far beyond its own membership, for the public at large probably does not make any distinction between members and nonmembers, and the latter would be under as great social pressure as the former to observe whatever standards a national body like this association had published.

CHAPTER XI

SUMMARY AND CONCLUSION

EXPANSION

The unprecedented growth of the association during this period is due to the conjunctivity of numerous factors. Among these factors is the use of promotion devices with which teachers and others had become familiar during the World War, including rivalry and compulsion. Many kinds of devices were effective in influencing behavior during the war period and immediately thereafter upon issues of national significance, and the association adopted one such issue, the creation of a national department of education. Sociologists have frequently noted the efficacy of such means of promotion as the association has used, including not only rivalry and compulsion, but the establishment of traditions, the utilization of personal prestige, the use of repeated direct and indirect suggestion for action, the appeal to the wish for public recognition and the wish for security, the discovery and definition of crises. Increased service to members has also been a factor in the expansion. The reorganization of the association brought an increase in membership as a by-product. The momentum achieved during the first part of the period being studied, atypical as it was because of the patriotically emotionalized elements in the situation, has been maintained during the latter part of the period through the continuance of all the promotion devices and all the services to members as well as through the implications which the very fact of great numbers carries with it as to professional acceptability.

Some classes of teachers are not reached by the promotion devices used. Moreover, membership induced through the use of artificial promotion devices is of less value to the association than membership based on occupational acculturation—a development of genuine appreciation of the values to be achieved through professional organization. Courses presenting these values to students in teachers colleges and normal schools would do much to develop a stable, permanent foundation of professional attitudes upon which to build an organization such as the National Education Association. The present is an opportune time to attempt to induce teacher-training institutions to include this kind of material in their curricula, for it is a period of transition from two-year to longer periods of training, and new materials of various kinds are being added.

Organizations of teachers who are quite highly specialized, and who for that reason are not deeply interested in a general organization such as this association, might find it advantageous to have their organizations integrated into this association on a basis that would leave them practically autonomous, but with executive and research service provided by one staff.

ORGANIZATION

Full governing authority in the association is held by a Representative Assembly acting under a Congressional charter. Delegates are chosen annually by affiliated groups which are of a political-geographic character rather than a special-interest character. An actual membership of more than a thousand and a potential membership of two thousand in this assembly render it incapable of functioning properly or effectively as a deliberative or legislative body, except upon the most general issues. The composition of the assembly is affected to some degree by the operation of two tendencies that are irrelevant to the functions to be performed, namely, the tendencies to choose as delegates (1) those whose traveling expenses are paid out of public funds, and (2) those whose vacation travels will take them to, or near, the convention city. About five-sixths of the delegates at any annual meeting are serving their first term and, because of their inexperience, are not fully competent to represent their groups effectively. The factor of size of group coupled with that of inexperience of the majority results in the adoption of motions and resolutions by passive assent to the proposals of leaders rather than by critical analysis on the part of the delegate body as a whole. Remedies for the foregoing defects would be (1) sharp reduction of number of delegates, (2) payment of delegates' convention expenses out of the funds of the association and affiliated groups, and (3) election of delegates for terms of more than one year.

Another problem in the scheme of organization is that of overlapping of representation, due to the fact that both state and local associations are directly affiliated with the national body and that in

Summary and Conclusion

many cases the "locals" are subsidiary to the state associations. Still another problem arises from the fact that members of the national body cannot have a voice in its affairs except by becoming members of affiliated bodies. In the interests of unity and simplicity of organization there should be a single fee admitting to membership in local, state, and national associations with the local being subsidiary to the state association and the state to the national body. There are indications that this desired end may be reached eventually, although, like most projects affecting groups that are already organized, it will no doubt require a relatively long time, with several intermediate adjustments, for its consummation. The present insecurity of the relationship called affiliation would be somewhat diminished if the entire membership of affiliated associations were to take part in the election of delegates and state directors, and if these were chosen for longer, overlapping terms. In order to insure representation of all specialized subgroups, departmental representation should supplement the present scheme of political-geographic representation.

The Board of Directors performs many of the legislative functions of the association, these being delegated to it by the Assembly. Members are elected annually and the average period of service on this board is less than two years. The Executive Committee might be composed almost entirely of inexperienced persons at a particular time, but a certain amount of continuity in its policies is assured through both official and informal interlocking of its membership and activities with those of the long-term Board of Trustees.

The association gives its departments a considerable degree of autonomy, and some of them are practically independent except for the fact that their executive functions are coördinated with those of the parent body. The creation of new departments is limited by: (1) a numerical rule, which is a crude measure of the importance of a specialized interest; and (2) a rule requiring the preparation of "constructive" programs, which puts a premium on conformity with the points of view of the leadership subgroups that define the word "constructive." The establishment of departments is an obvious adjustment to the diversity of interest within the membership of the association without splitting into separate sectarian groups.

The executive staff is a unified body of paid specialists organized in line with accepted administrative principles. The executive secretary rightly has a dominant position in the association. The association should take account of this dominance, however, through the exercise of considerable care in the selection of the board that chooses this officer; through the creation of a membership forum in *The Journal* for the full discussion of executive policies; and through provisions for assuring longer terms of office, and hence more intelligent analysis of association affairs, in the Assembly, the Board of Directors, and the Executive Committee.

Committees and commissions are created for activities in limited areas within which the regular leadership groups cannot function effectively. The size and geographic derivation as well as the personnel of these special-function subgroups should be determined on a basis that is relevant to the function to be performed. In the technical matters of fact-finding, classification, and analysis, these subgroups properly make use of the services of the trained staff in the Division of Research.

LEADERSHIP

In the official leadership of the association, women play a subordinate but an increasing part. The factors which promote male leadership within the association are the same factors that promote male leadership outside the association, not only in education but in other fields as well. Likewise, from the professional positions in which most authority and prestige are concentrated come most of the association's office-holders. The fact of short terms for elected leaders would justify the a priori assumption that the leadership quite promptly and accurately reflects the will of the membership, but this is not necessarily true because of the disproportionate influence which a few members of the Assembly and the Board of Directors may exert, by reason of their somewhat permanent place in these bodies and their professional prestige, upon the members who are new and especially upon those from the lower professional levels.

On the other hand, this relatively permanent element in the leadership of the association may be assumed to promote stability and consistency in policy, in proportion to its active participation in the affairs of the association.

ACTIVITIES

The "general sessions" at annual conventions represent in reality a carefully controlled forum for communicating, to members and to the general public, information and points of view approved by the leaders. The mode of communication is through addresses delivered by persons of prestige. In addition to formal expressions, these in-

Summary and Conclusion 159

clude materials classified as interpretation, inspiration, stimulation, educational information, general information, discussion of affairs of the collective group, discussion of matters affecting the welfare of members, communication of subgroup points of view, communication from outside groups, and general and educational philosophy. The situation at these general sessions is "inspiring," that is, it is such as to magnify the members' feeling of importance in the social order. Their behavior, for example, their approval or disapproval of a proposal, in this crowd situation is not a safe guide in matters of association policy, either as to principles to be approved or as to activities. These sessions probably have considerable value, however, (1) in unifying not only the members of the association but to some extent the entire teaching population; (2) in providing a means of reorientation of members in a rapidly changing professional world, so far as the addresses deal with current professional matters; and (3) in communicating effectively with the general public upon educational matters, because of the news value attaching to large national gatherings. Whether they have sufficient value to justify their cost in money, time, and energy, in view of certain changed and changing conditions, is open to question.

In many instances the formal resolutions adopted at the annual conventions are typical crowd products, products of the personal interest of a temporary leader or small number of leaders and the undeliberated assent of an inert or suggestible majority of the Assembly delegates. Certain undesirable possibilities arise from the present method of adoption of these formal pronouncements, namely, scattering of energy and resources, divisions within the membership, and loss of professional and public confidence in the association. It is proposed in this study that the number of official declarations be limited to the number to which the association can give active and effective support, and that those to be supported at a particular period be determined by a ranking or preferential voting scheme which would yield a consensus of the judgment of "professional" members as distinct from casual members.

The executive divisions perform a great and an increasing share of the actual work of the association. They are not limited to the carrying out of the specific instructions of the leadership subgroups, but they are permitted to assume active leadership functions to a certain extent. Indefinite tenure, with long terms for division heads as the rule, will tend to increase the influence of the executive staff, both within and without the association, and will tend to promote consistency and stability in association policy.

There is no objective evidence as to the effectiveness of the activities of the association on behalf of the establishment of a Federal Department of Education. Opposition to the proposal has had time to become organized, and there is less public sentiment in favor of attacking problems on a national scale than was the case a few years ago, both of these factors lessening the chances of immediate success in the enterprise. However, changes in the social and economic and political life of the country are bringing about the necessity of increased national control in these fields, and education, in its organization and support, should ideally be kept abreast of these other fields. Even in the absence of a prospect of formal success, the Legislative Division's activities are to be approved sociologically if they result in diminishing the "lag" between these general social-economic-political developments and educational conditions. On the other hand, to attempt to secure a change in educational organization and support in advance of conditions in these other fields demanding such a change, is futile, and the association should give careful consideration to all factors in the situation before determining its future legislative activity.

The association engages in extensive and complex intra-group and extra-group communication. Its techniques are of kinds likely to be effective. Its present practice is to communicate to the members through *The Journal* only those points of view favorable to present leadership and policies. This may be the means of perpetuating group weakness, shortsightedness, or error. The organization's long-time advancement, if it is to be assured, must be based upon critically analyzed, sound principles. It could lose nothing, and it might gain much, by letting *The Journal* be used as a forum for the free discussion of present and future policies.

The association, through its research division, gathers and tabulates data on a great variety of subjects of importance to the association and to teachers in general. This division is the active agency through which many association committees work. In view of the association's national and general character, perhaps its primary research obligation should be to make a continuous survey and summary and synthesis of researches being conducted by other agencies,[1]

---

[1] Unless this service should be adequately performed by some other appropriate agency such as the United States Office of Education.

Summary and Conclusion

even though, because of its limited resources, it might have to abandon its own research activities in order to undertake this other service.

A complete coördination of activities of divisions and departments, such as is found in the case of the Division of Administrative Service and the Department of Superintendence, represents a policy which might be advantageously extended to include other departments.

The various governing bodies engage in activities of great variety. With the exception of the Board of Trustees, they do not have their spheres of action clearly defined in the constitution and by-laws. Whereas this lack of clear definition of function results in considerable overlapping, it is probably actually advantageous in an organization in which the larger bodies cannot meet oftener than once or twice a year. Consistency in policy among the various leadership subgroups is promoted by constitutional and extra-constitutional interlocking.

CONFLICT

The association has been largely successful in avoiding internal conflict, this being not only due to definite attempts to avoid it but also to a selective process which causes persons of conflict temperament to stay out of a non-fighting group; also to a diminution in the conflict, outside the association, among various professional subgroups; and to the further fact that those who find themselves in disagreement with a major policy of the association tend not to become or to remain members.

Although it cannot be called a "fighting" group, it does engage in controversies with its natural opponents and it has made conflict a somewhat specialized function. Except in response to attacks made upon it or upon its prominent members, its conflict pronouncements are mild and conciliatory in tone. Conciliation is to be interpreted as a procedure adopted in anticipation of conflict, however, and although it is impossible to place a value upon it as compared with other procedures, it is obvious that it is highly important in the case of an organization so situated that it must secure the aid of many organizations if it is to promote its own enterprises successfully.

COÖPERATION

The complexity of the organization, with its numerous special-interest and special-function subgroups, bears witness to an extensive and complex internal coöperation. The association seeks and grants formal coöperation with other organizations quite widely, but in most instances the coöperative relationship is not very active or vital. Moreover, its procedures in establishing these relationships give rise to the possibility of scattered energy and resources and even of the appearance of sponsorship of measures which at a particular time it no longer endorses. It should create a machinery for very careful consideration of proposals for coöperation in advance of their establishment, accepting only those to which its current major policies are closely related, and subjecting them to constant and critical review to determine the propriety of continuing, modifying, or terminating them.

CONTROL

The association has not concerned itself with extensive control of its members. It is nonexclusive. Because of its size it cannot be expected to become the primary agency for the investigation of violation of standards. If it should formulate a code of professional conduct by a careful consensus procedure, as it has recently undertaken to do, this group could no doubt make such a code somewhat effective, by reason of its prestige as a national organization, through acquainting the general public with its provisions, and through securing its inclusion in the curricula of teacher-training institutions. If a code is vigorously promoted and if local and state and special associations proceed to apply it within their own areas, the national association will undoubtedly be called upon to interpret the code in doubtful or marginal cases referred to it by these smaller professional groups.

PROBLEMS SUGGESTED BY THIS STUDY

The National Education Association during the period of this study may be characterized as an organization of professional and casual teachers; largely feminine in membership; largely masculine in leadership; nonexclusive; opportunistically promoted; rapidly expanding; nonspecialized; nonpolitical; nonmilitant; coöperative in spirit; relatively insecure; without clearly defined objectives; nominally, but not functionally, representative in government; possessing effective executive machinery; mainly secondary in the contacts which it provides among its members; without extensive control over its members; without a technique of self-criticism.

These characteristics have been disclosed in the present study, and so far as they imply defects in the organization, remedies inherent

Summary and Conclusion 163

in the situations themselves have been pointed out. The objectives of the study do not include reform of the association, so there has been no attempt to elaborate these suggestions and there is no inclination to defend them as possessing final validity. Even with regard to the general sociological interpretations, no finality is claimed, for the obvious reason that, as indicated at the outset, this study had taken account only: (1) of the organization and activities of the association as a whole, not of the departments; (2) of the wishes, attitudes, and personal evaluations of leaders and members, so far as they are manifested in overt behavior; and (3) of factors and conditions in the social milieu that are so effectively expressed as to produce overt behavior on the part of the group, omitting those which are themselves inarticulate or which fail to produce an articulate response on the part of the group. Studies of the kinds implied in these recognized omissions must be completed in order to provide anything like an adequate sociological analysis of the National Education Association.

Incidentally, numerous problems for research, of practical importance to educators in the United States, are suggested by the present study. Among these are:

1. What is the kind and what the extent of the influence of the National Education Association upon American education? Upon particular divisions of the educational field, e.g., the elementary field, the junior high school? Upon school administration? Upon the curriculum? Upon adult education? Upon vocational education?

2. What has been and is the extent of the influence of this association upon teacher training? Upon conditions of work—teaching load, tenure, retirement, leave, wage? Upon teachers' professional attitudes?

3. What is the influence of this association upon other groups? Upon the state associations of teachers? Upon the American Federation of Teachers? Upon the Association of University Professors? Upon the American Federation of Labor? Upon the National Congress of Parents and Teachers?

4. What is the social distance and what is the extent of divergent professional points of view as among specialized groups of teachers in America, for example, vocational teachers, English teachers in high schools, rural teachers, college teachers? How do these factors condition the possibility, the desirability, the extent, and the degree of

success of integration of these professional subgroups into one inclusive association?

5. What is the relation between the size and prestige of the National Education Association on the one hand and the social status of teachers in the United States on the other hand? How widely and how favorably is the association known? Does membership in it improve a teacher's status?

6. What is the relative influence, upon a national legislator, of social pressure exerted by a national association as compared to social pressure exerted by a state association of a similar kind in his own state?

7. In causing teachers to join the National Education Association, what is the relative strength of compulsion from superiors, rivalry with staffs of other schools, professional values to be secured, partisanship with regard to issues favored by the association? If a teacher joins the association because of the use of artificial promotion devices rather than because of professional interest, to what extent does the fact of membership develop professional interest?

8. If courses dealing with professional organization, including the obligation and the values of membership, are to be included in the curricula of teachers colleges and normal schools, what are the specific associations, or at least the *kinds* of organizations, to be endorsed as worthy of the primary interest of prospective teachers?

CONCLUSION: PRACTICAL RECOMMENDATIONS

Since reform of the National Education Association is not an objective of the present study, and since the study presents only a part of what would constitute a complete sociological analysis of the association, it must be evident that no general, sweeping recommendations may properly be made. Perhaps the only general proposal that may be made with propriety is that additional studies be undertaken to supplement the present one.

However, the data presented are believed to furnish an adequate basis for recommendation *as to certain limited aspects* of the association's organization and activities with which this study definitely deals. Therefore, in addition to proposals for research upon the problems just cited and proposals for a complete sociological analysis of the National Education Association, the following practical recommendations, which emerge quite logically from the study, are presented:

Summary and Conclusion

1. That, in promotion of expansion of membership, more use be made of programs of occupational acculturation.

2. That the size of the Representative Assembly be sharply reduced.

3. That provision be made for payment of expenses of members of the Representative Assembly from the funds of the association and affiliated and subsidiary groups.

4. That delegates to the Representative Assembly and members of the Board of Directors be elected for terms of more than one year, with provision for overlapping of terms.

5. That provision be made for the representation of departments in the Representative Assembly.

6. That state directors be elected by state organizations of teachers.

7. That provision be made for longer terms and overlapping terms of office for members of the Executive Committee.

8. That as soon as possible the "affiliated" local and state associations be included as integral parts of the national association.

9. That *The Journal* be used as a membership forum for discussion of association policies.

10. That all committees and commissions be created on bases relevant to the functions which they are to perform.

11. That all fact-finding committees and commissions make use of the services of the Research Division of the association.

12. That a careful study be made to determine the values to the association and to the teaching profession of the "general sessions" at the time of the annual convention, as compared with the values that might be secured from the same expenditure for other purposes.

13. That the association limit the number of projects endorsed or undertaken at a particular time to the number that it can support effectively at that time.

14. That the projects to be undertaken or supported by the association be determined by a referendum to the "professional" members of the association.

15. That the executive staff be permitted to continue in its dominant position in the association, under the safeguards provided by longer, overlapping terms of office in the Representative Assembly, Board of Directors, and Executive Committee, and by the establishment of a membership forum in *The Journal*.

16. That the kind and extent of activities designed to secure the

establishment of a Federal Department of Education be determined by the principle of avoidance of "lag" between social-economic-political conditions and educational conditions.

17. That this association undertake, as its primary research activity, a continuing survey and summary and synthesis of researches conducted by other educational agencies unless this service is performed by some other responsible and effective national agency.

18. That formal coöperative relationships with other groups be established only after careful study of all factors involved and that these relationships be subjected to a constant and critical review.

19. That the association promote the formulation and observance of a code of ethics for teachers.

SUPPLEMENT

THE ASSOCIATION AND THE WORLD WAR [1]

The first reaction of the association to the World War was one of internationalism and anti-militarism. The 1915 convention was held at Oakland, California, August 16 to 27, in connection with the Panama-Pacific International Exposition, and was in the nature of an International Congress on Education as had been decided by the Board of Directors of the association two years earlier. Thirty nations were represented by officially accredited delegates, by representatives from educational associations, or by speakers on the program. In the resolutions adopted, this gathering expressed the conviction that our systems of education had been shown ineffective by the breakdown of civilization in Europe. This declaration is worth quoting at length:

> Perhaps no greater work lies ahead of the school, in all lands and nations, than that of setting to work in an earnest endeavor to build up a more enduring type of civilization. We have made great progress in industry, commerce, and scientific work, but little as yet in establishing justice, goodwill, and the reign of law among nations. Our instruction, aside from those fundamental tool subjects which underlie all educational work, has been based upon too narrow an outlook. Nationalism has been pushed to the front and emphasized rather than international justice and good-will. The heroes of each nation's history have been those who have done the greatest injury to other nations and who have killed the greatest number of foreigners rather than those who have conferred the greatest benefits on mankind. Our geography has related too much to the position, growth, and commercial progress of our own nation and too little to our relations with other peoples. Our patriotism has been too much concerned with our rights and too little with our obligations; too much with securing advantages for ourselves, and too little with the extension of international justice and goodwill. There has been too much talk in all nations of "national honor" and "rallying to the defense of the flag," and too little of national obligations and responsibilities. The discipline of our schools has been too much the discipline of the intellect and the body, untempered by large conceptions as to justice and good-will among men.
> ... In particular the school histories need to be rewritten and the teach-

[1] See pp. 11-13 of the present study.

ing in history and geography in the schools needs to be entirely redirected. . . . The emphasis now placed on wars should be shifted to the gains to civilization made in the intervals between wars, . . . broadening of the work in civics and morals, . . . substitution of international tribunals and the reign of law and order for the present appeal to brute force and so-called national honor, . . . development of an international patriotism, . . . world interests, world civilization, world statesmanship, and world friendship and good-will in place of the present narrow nationalism. . . .

The association reaffirms its approval of the American School Peace League, the organization of Peace Leagues among pupils, the observance of Peace Day, May 18, and the dissemination of literature bearing on international relations. . . . The association deplores any attempt to militarize this country. It again declares against the establishment of compulsory military training in the schools, on the ground that this is reactionary and inconsistent with American ideals and standards.

. . . The presence of military and naval attachés in all embassies and legations emphasizes the least desirable factors of international relations. . . . Each of the national governments . . . should be urged to appoint educational attachés . . . to their legations and embassies in foreign countries.[2]

It would be difficult to draft a more sweeping declaration than this in support of a peace program for the schools and the nation, and in opposition to a militaristic program. The fact that a secretary of the American School Peace League was a member of the Committee on Resolutions is worthy of record. The statement brought forth widespread comment from general and educational periodicals and caused them as well as some of the leaders in the association itself to be on the alert in regard to the kind of resolutions to be adopted the following year at the convention held in New York City. In that year, the following statement was issued: [3]

Resolved, that the National Education Association give expression again to the consciousness that the school is an institution developed by society to conserve the well-being of humanity, and that on this solid foundation all subordinate aims and uses of the school should be made to rest. Assembled as it is in a time of world-wide disturbance, doubt, and uncertainty, and of consequent national concern, the association affirms its unswerving adherence to the unchanging principles of justice between persons and between nations; it affirms its belief that the instruction in the school should tend to furnish the mind with the knowledge of the arts and sciences on which the prosperity of the nations rests and to incline the will of men and nations toward acts of peace; it declares its devotion to America and American ideals and recognizes the priority of the claims of our beloved country on our property, our minds, our hearts, and our lives. It records its conviction that the true policy to be followed, both by the school and by the

[2] *Add. and Proc.,* 1915, pp. 25-30.
[3] *Add. and Proc.,* 1916, pp. 27-28.

nation which it serves, is to keep the American public school free from sectarian influences, partisan politics, and disputed public policies, that it may remain unimpaired in its power to serve the whole people. While it recognizes that the community, or the state, may introduce such elements of military training into the schools as may seem wise and prudent, yet it believes that such training should be strictly educational in its aim and organization, and that military ends should not be permitted to pervert the educational purposes and practices of the school.

Undoubtedly, several factors entered into the situation to cause the association to make a public declaration which differed so markedly from that adopted in 1915. There was considerable agitation of the military preparedness issue on the part of the public at large. The convention was addressed by such leaders on both sides of the question as William Jennings Bryan and Major General Leonard Wood, and the members were showered with circulars that had been printed by various militaristic and pacifistic organizations. The newspapers carried editorials dealing with the question. The fact was that the issue was alive and that the general public as well as the educational public was sharply divided upon it. If not actually favoring military training, the convention seemed "acquiescent and receptive" to the idea, according to some observers. It even failed to follow up its broad, constructive proposal of a year earlier concerning the removal of military emphasis in textbooks.[4] Its position was variously described by the New York newspapers as a "straddle," a "compromise," a victory for the militarists, an "about face."[5] It is possible that the rank and file of the teachers attending the convention were indifferent to the issue or felt themselves uninformed and therefore unable to pass judgment and that they would have approved any resolution dealing with the question which their leaders presented to them.[6]

When the association met in convention in 1917, the United States had entered the war. The resolutions adopted supported the war program whole-heartedly and in detail, and gave conclusive proof that the members were now reacting as patriots, as nationalists, not as international idealists. To quote:

The National Education Association . . . recognizes that the first duty of the hour is whole-hearted national loyalty. Our supreme wish is to give

[4] Lane, Winthrop D., "Teaching and Military Training," *Survey*, XXXVI (July 15, 1916), pp. 418-19.
[5] "The National Education Association and Military Training in the Schools," *School and Society*, IV (July 16, 1916), pp. 102-6.
[6] Lane, Winthrop D., *op. cit.*, pp. 418-19.

the fullest measure of service for the sacred cause of our country and our allies, in defense of democracy and righteousness.

We pledge to President Wilson and the national administration and to governors and other authorities of our respective states, that we will conduct all educational affairs committed to our care in this spirit, putting aside for the present the consideration of all other questions, however important.

We rejoice that the young men and women of our country have manifested such a splendid spirit of patriotic devotion to the national cause. The records of our secondary schools, colleges, and universities give proof that the American educational system has not failed to inculcate the spirit of patriotism. We are proud of the work that our young people are doing in army, navy, training camps, hospitals, and Red Cross service.

... In order that the greatest possible efficiency may be immediately secured [it is recommended that there should be] revision of courses of study, improvement of methods of instruction, alterations in the lengths and dates of school terms, shortening of vacations and holidays, adaptation of school days with provision for part-time work, the maintenance of continuation schools, the wider use of school plants, prompt organization and further development of industrial and other forms of vocational work ... physical education, including medical inspection for all children in all schools. ...

In technical institutions, colleges, and universities, where young men are of suitable age, we recommend that the government give every encouragement to genuine military training, ample in scope and practical in character.

The nation needs the benefits of genuine thrift and conservation of all resources. To this end we recommend that all schools and institutions make definite provision for the teaching of these practical virtues.

... We urge that patriotism be taught by every teacher of whatever grade. ...

... We pledge ... that we will work with entire devotion for the establishment of triumphant peace after victory, a peace to be administered by a "Veritable League of Honor," an inclusive league of nations, founded upon the principle of national loyalty extended into world citizenship.[7]

The resolutions of the 1918 convention were no less fervid in their expression of devotion to the nation's cause, and they approved what would now be considered somewhat extreme policies in the matter of the use of the English language, the universal teaching of patriotism, and various other matters. Excerpts from the formal statement adopted by the convention follow:

The National Education Association ... recognizes that the first great business of the nation is the winning of the war, and to this end pledges the fullest measure of service and sacrifice for the sacred cause of our country, of democracy, and of humanity.

[7] *Add. and Proc.*, 1917, pp. 26-27.

Supplement

... With peculiar satisfaction, the association points to the fact that 750,000 teachers and twenty-two million pupils have supported loyally every plan and purpose of President Wilson and Congress in their masterful leadership in honorable warfare for a just cause and a decisive victory.

[College military units are approved.]

The association demands the teaching of patriotism by every teacher from the kindergarten to the university, and the employment of only those teachers who are loyal to our national ideals. It urges that all teachers, as soldiers of the common good, take the oath of allegiance. The association further demands that all instruction in the schools of the nation be conducted in the English language.

... In the emergency that now exists, the association urges that all the manhood and womanhood of the United States be conscripted for selective service.

[The association expresses confidence in the national administration, and especially in President Woodrow Wilson.] [8]

Here, it would seem, is conclusive evidence that so far as the resolutions may be said to reflect the views of the members, the association whole-heartedly and vigorously supported the war program after the United States had entered the war, but that up to the time when the general public had become aroused upon some of the issues, the members of the association were either ardent supporters of peace and internationalism or they were so indifferent that they permitted a minority to place them on record as wholly anti-militaristic and not at all nationalistic. If the organization was really as peace-loving as it appeared in 1915, if it had firm, emotionalized conviction on the subject of all things military, there was no reason for it to modify its stand a year later. The country had not yet entered the war. It was still possible to be at once a patriot and an advocate of peace. The only development was that the issue had become one of public concern through the agitation of political and other leaders. In this situation the association retreated from its advanced position of 1915 and assumed a position not likely to cause it to be violently attacked from any quarter. As stated earlier, the majority of those attending the 1916 convention may even then have been so indifferent, or may have felt themselves so incapable of passing judgment, that they would have assented to any proposition submitted by the Committee on Resolutions, but at least the leaders, the officers, and committee members, facing certain violent opposition if they repeated their statement of the year before, did not repeat it either in substance or in tone.

[8] *Add. and Proc.*, 1918, pp. 23-26

During the war years, 1917 and 1918, as already pointed out, in their resolutions the members reacted as patriots and not as an occupational group. In this they were in line with other groups—all other classes in American society.

APPENDIX

In 1910 Carter Alexander made a study of teachers' associations under the title *Some Present Aspects of the Work of Teachers' Voluntary Associations in the United States* (Contributions to Education, No. 36, Bureau of Publications, Teachers College, Columbia University, New York). Here are presented brief excerpts from that study, all dealing with the National Education Association.[1]

Nature of the Association

Of the national associations, we find only one that is practically universal in membership and general in its work—the National Education Association. This is indeed so general that it does not limit its membership to teachers but is open to "teachers and all who are actively associated with the management of educational institutions." The association itself is not really one large unified body, but is a rather loose association of practically independent and highly specialized sections. The Department of Superintendence, with its meeting carefully put in February or March so as to miss the general meeting in the summer, is practically a department of the association only in name and a few details of management. [pp. 5-6]

Sections and Departments

In the National Education Association, the opinion has frequently been advanced that there are too many sections and a consequent waste of energy, but little has been done to remedy the defect. The Board of Directors in 1909 did agree to limit the number of departments to nine but this agreement does not seem to have been followed, the number of departments for 1910 being eighteen. Besides, this move may in a sense be only an indication of greater specialization; among the reasons advanced for the reduction of the departments was one that several classes of teachers, such as the kindergartners and the art teachers, prefer to get their associational experience in separate associations so that it is unnecessary to try to arrange special departments for them.

Further indications are seen in numerous adverse criticisms in the last few years leveled at the National Education Association, most of them accusing it of failure to keep itself a truly national body, representative of all educational interests, and some of them going so far as to predict early decay for it. [p. 13]

. . . In many respects the best plan seems to be that of general associations

---

[1] Headings used are not quoted.

of reasonable size with plenty of sections. These sections could then elect delegates to representative councils covering larger territories as is already done in several of the state councils of education, only many of these are not representative of all the interests concerned. This plan might be extended up to associations that would cover the whole country. If this were done, it would be possible to have a truly national association, getting out a truly representative yearbook of incalculable value—a consummation devoutly to be wished though at present far from being attained. [p. 27]

Legislative Activity

The National Education Association has attempted and is attempting very little in the way of legislation for the reason that in the United States education has not heretofore been generally considered a matter for national legislative action. There is no specific provision for influencing legislation and no direct reference to the idea in any of the structural arrangements of the association. What little it has done has in the main been confined to the passing of rather futile resolutions and the appointing of short-lived committees on the United States Bureau of Education, the establishment of a National University, and National Aid to Education. All these questions have been considered in their recurring cycles within a year or so, but the usual differences of opinion and failure to take definite and continued action regarding them have led to nothing of importance. [pp. 28-29]

Economic Betterment of Teachers

The National Education Association has never concerned itself much with efforts to advance the material welfare of teachers. It did have a committee in 1877 to formulate a protest against reducing teachers' salaries during the financial depression then existing; it has had occasional addresses on teachers' salaries, and it authorized a Special Committee on Salaries, Tenure of Office and Pensions, in 1903, which made a very valuable report to the National Council of Education, in 1905. But on the whole, the National Education Association has apparently "thought it was beneath the dignity of the Association" to talk about the "money basis of education."

The movement for pensions is, on the whole, very recent. The National Education Association in 1891 passed the following resolution:

"Justice as well as the best public service requires the retirement and pensioning of teachers after a service of thirty years, and upon carefully devised conditions. We recommend the enactment of laws in the states to permit and regulate the retirement and pensioning of professional teachers."

While more permanent tenure of office has long been set up as an ideal by the associations, it is only lately that they have begun to work for it very definitely. As yet little has been accomplished. The National Education Association published the report of the Committee on Salaries, Tenure of

Office and Pensions of Public School Teachers in 1905, which devoted some attention to the subject. [pp. 49, 51, 52]

The report (referred to in the preceding quotation) covered exhaustively the following topics:

Salaries of teachers in practically all towns over 8,000
Salaries of teachers in selected towns of less than 8,000
Salaries of teachers in typical ungraded rural schools
Funds for the payment of teachers' salaries
Minimum salary laws
Earnings in teaching and in other occupations
Purchasing power of salaries in different localities
Tenure of office of teachers
Pensions for teachers [pp. 61-62]

The Place of Women in the Association

In the National Education Association so far as specific institutional recognition of them is concerned, women members have been practically non-entities. Until the election of Mrs. Ella Flagg Young to the presidency for 1911, no woman ever served in an executive office in the association. The membership of the association is a difficult thing to handle accurately, but estimates of the proportion of women in it are from seventy-five per cent up, so far as mere registration is concerned. But of the officers of the general association for 1909-10, no woman served as a trustee or on the executive committee, and there was only one woman vice-president out of eleven. Of the state directors there were two women out of forty-nine members, and in the Council of Education seventeen out of one hundred twenty members.

The same state of affairs appears in the case of the departmental officers. Although the women have a fourth of these, fourteen out of fifty-seven, inspection indicates that this ratio is to be discounted. They have only two presidencies and these are in the kindergarten and women's organizations departments where there is not competition with men; they have five vice-presidencies which are purely honorary positions; the remaining seven offices are secretaryships which, while necessary, are not generally counted places of any great importance or demanding much more than faithful and persistent attention to details and carrying out the instructions of other people. Nine of the departments have no women officials whatever.

Again the same thing is seen in the programs. On the program of the general sessions of the main association appears one woman out of fourteen speakers; in the Department of Superintendence, two out of sixty. Of the departmental programs three have no women whatever, only one (the department of women's organizations) has more women than men, only three others have half the number or over of women; the median percentage of women is but ten. [pp. 69-70]

Many women join state associations and even the National Education Association practically under compulsion from their superintendents who are enthusiastic for a large attendance at the associations; such women naturally care nothing about the associations and have no intention whatever of attending them unless forced to do so by their superintendents or boards of education. Under these circumstances there is some reason for believing that there is no real discrimination against women in the associations.

Another cause for this seeming discrimination is probably the short stay of women in the teaching profession. The people who appear on the programs of the associations and gradually work up to the offices are naturally those who attend year after year. Women who do not intend to teach long make little effort to go to these associations, although, as before mentioned, they may be practically forced into taking out membership. The few women who do occupy prominent places in the association are those who attend regularly year after year, and their names appear in the offices in the same way. Many women teachers are also prevented from attending the associations because of low salaries, although they may take out memberships because they are forced to do so or because they desire copies of the proceedings.

. . . Even if, on the whole, women at present occupy a very subordinate position in teachers' associations, still, by a slow and gradual evolution, they have made great progress since the associations first organized. . . . Within the last few years there have been some activities of women, which, while they have not as yet produced much in the way of tangible results, are nevertheless indicative of future lines of development. [pp. 76-77]

BIBLIOGRAPHY [1]

ALEXANDER, CARTER. *Some Present Aspects of the Work of Teachers' Voluntary Associations in the United States.* Contributions to Education, No. 36. Bureau of Publications, Teachers College, Columbia University, New York, 1910.

ALLPORT, F. H. *Social Psychology.* Houghton Mifflin Co., Boston, 1924.

BERNARD, L. L. "The Psychological Foundations of Society." In *An Introduction to Sociology* by Davis, Barnes, and Others (Part III). D. C. Heath & Co., Boston, 1927.

BOGARDUS, E. S. *Fundamentals of Social Psychology.* The Century Co., New York, 1924.

BOGARDUS, E. S. "Social Distance and Its Origins." *Journal of Applied Sociology,* Vol. IX, pp. 216-26, January, 1925.

BRAINARD, P. P. "First Step Toward a United Organization of Teachers." *School and Society,* Vol. XI, pp. 217-20, February 21, 1920.

CHAMBERS, GEORGE GAILEY. "Codes of Ethics for the Teaching Profession." *Annals of the American Academy of Political and Social Science.* Vol. CI, No. 190, pp. 121-27, May, 1922.

CHILD, C. M. "Biological Foundations of Social Integration." *Publications of the American Sociological Society,* Vol. XXII, pp. 26-42, 1928.

COOLEY, C. H. "The Life Study Method as Applied to Rural Social Research." *Publications of the American Sociological Society,* Vol. XXIII, pp. 248-54, 1929.

COOLEY, C. H. *Human Nature and the Social Order.* Charles Scribner's Sons, New York, 1922.

COOLEY, C. H. *Social Organization.* Charles Scribner's Sons, New York, 1924.

COUNTS, G. S. *School and Society in Chicago.* Harcourt, Brace and Company, New York, 1928.

COUNTS, G. S. "The Social Status of Occupations." *School Review,* Vol. XXXIII, pp. 16-27, January, 1925.

CURTIS, W. C. "Unionization from the Standpoint of a University Teacher." *Educational Review,* Vol. LX, pp. 91-105, September, 1920.

"The Department of Superintendence at Atlantic City," (Editorial) *School and Society,* Vol. XIII, pp. 331-37, March 19, 1921.

ELLWOOD, C. A. *The Psychology of Human Society.* D. Appleton and Company, New York, 1925.

---

[1] This bibliography includes the selected references cited in the study, with the exception of the publications of the National Education Association itself. These latter materials constitute the raw data with which the study deals and therefore would not be included properly in a list of references.

ELLWOOD, C. A. "Recent Developments in Sociology." In *Recent Developments in the Social Sciences*, edited by E. C. Hayes (Chapter I). J. B. Lippincott Company, Philadelphia, 1927.

ENGELHARDT, F. W. "Organization of Teachers." *School and Society*, Vol. XI, pp. 468-69, April 17, 1920.

GEHLKE, C. E. "The Use and Limitations of Statistics in Sociological Research." *Publications of the American Sociological Society*, Vol. XXI, 1927.

GIDDINGS, F. H. *The Scientific Study of Human Society*. University of North Carolina Press, Chapel Hill, 1924.

GIDDINGS, F. H. *Studies in the Theory of Human Society*. The Macmillan Co., New York, 1922.

GRANRUD, JOHN. *The Organization and Objectives of State Teachers Associations*. Contributions to Education, No. 234. Bureau of Publications, Teachers College, Columbia University, New York, 1926.

A Handbook of Educational Associations and Foundations in the United States. Bulletin, 1926, No. 16. United States Bureau of Education, Washington, D. C.

HAYES, E. C. *Introduction to the Study of Sociology*. D. Appleton and Company, New York, 1923.

JACOBS, P. P. *German Sociology*. Ph.D. Thesis, Columbia University, New York, 1909.

JONES, OLIVE M. "The Nation's Teachers." *School and Society*, Vol. XX, pp. 1-9, July 5, 1924.

KELLER, A. G. *Societal Evolution*. The Macmillan Co., New York, 1915.

KULP, D. H., II. *Outlines of the Sociology of Human Behavior*. A. G. Seiler, 1224 Amsterdam Ave., New York, 1926.

KULP, D. H., II. *Country Life in South China*. Bureau of Publications, Teachers College, Columbia University, New York, 1925.

LANDIS, BENSON Y. *Professional Codes*. Contributions to Education, No. 267. Bureau of Publications, Teachers College, Columbia University, New York, 1927.

LANE, WINTHROP D. "Teaching and Military Training." *Survey*, Vol. XXVI, pp. 418-19, July 15, 1916.

LEHMAN, HARVEY C., AND WITTY, PAUL A. "Some Suggestions for Making Teaching a Profession." *Educational Review*, Vol. LXXIV, pp. 258-69, December, 1927.

LINDEMAN, E. C. *Social Discovery*. Republic Publishing Co., New York, 1925.

LIPPMANN, WALTER. *Public Opinion*. Harcourt, Brace and Company, New York, 1922.

MORRIS, WILSON C. "The American Association of Teachers." *School and Society*, Vol. VIII, pp. 635-40, November 30, 1918.

"The National Education Association" (Editorial). *School Review*, Vol. XXXI, pp. 481-83, September, 1923.

"The National Education Association and Military Training in the Schools" (Editorial). *School and Society*, Vol. IV, pp. 102-6, July 16, 1916.

OGBURN, W. F. *Social Change*. The Viking Press, New York, 1928.

OGG, F. A., AND RAY, P. O. *Introduction to American Government*. The Century Co., New York, 1928.

"Organization of the Teaching Profession" (Editorial). *School and Society,* Vol. IX, pp. 117-18, January 25, 1919.

ORTSCHILD, VIOLA. "Grade Teachers Associations." *Oregon Teachers Monthly,* Vol. XXI, pp. 14-19, September, 1916.

PALMER, VIVIEN M. *Field Studies in Sociology.* University of Chicago Press, Chicago, 1928.

PARK, R. E., AND BURGESS, E. W. *Introduction to the Science of Sociology.* University of Chicago Press, Chicago, 1924.

QUEEN, S. A. "Round Table on the Case-Study Method of Sociological Research." *Publications of the American Sociological Society,* Vol. XXII, pp. 225-27, 1928.

"The Reorganized National Education Association" (Editorial). *School Review,* Vol. XXVIII, p. 481-86, September, 1920.

"The Reorganized National Education Association" (Editorial). *School Review,* Vol. XXIX, pp. 481-83, September, 1921.

RITTER, W. E., AND BAILEY, EDNA W. *The Organismal Conception, Its Place in Science and Its Bearing on Philosophy.* University of California Press, Berkeley, 1928.

Ross, E. A. *Principles of Sociology.* The Century Co., New York, 1921.

Ross, E. A. *Social Control.* The Macmillan Co., New York, 1901.

RUSSELL, JAMES E. "Organization of Teachers," *Educational Review,* Vol. LX, pp. 129-35, September, 1920.

RYAN, W. CARSON, JR. "The National Education Association at Boston." *School and Society,* Vol. XVI, pp. 57-64, July 15, 1922.

SHANKLAND, S. D. "State Secretaries Meet." *Educational Review,* Vol. LXXIII, pp. 77-78, February, 1927.

SIDIS, B. *The Psychology of Suggestion.* D. Appleton and Company, New York, 1901.

SIMMEL, G. "The Sociology of Conflict" (translated from the German by Albion W. Small). *American Journal of Sociology,* Vol. IX, p. 490, 1903-1904.

SMITH, W. R. *Principles of Educational Sociology.* Houghton Mifflin Co., Boston, 1928.

SNEDDEN, DAVID. "The Professional Improvement of Teachers and Teaching Through Organization." *School and Society,* Vol. X, pp. 531-39, November 8, 1919.

SPYKMAN, N. J. *The Social Theory of Georg Simmel.* University of Chicago Press, Chicago, 1925.

"Teachers' Salaries and the Wages for Unskilled Labor" (Editorial). *School and Society,* Vol. XI, pp. 176-77, February 7, 1920.

THOMAS, W. I. "The Behavior Pattern and the Situation." *Publications of the American Sociological Society,* Vol. XXII, pp. 1-13, 1928.

THOMAS, W. I. *The Unadjusted Girl.* Little, Brown and Co., Boston, 1925.

THOMAS, W. I., AND ZNANIECKI, F. *The Polish Peasant in Europe and America.* Vol. I. Alfred A. Knopf, New York, 1927.

VINCENT, G. E. "The Rivalry of Social Groups." *American Journal of Sociology,* Vol. XVI, pp. 471-84, 1910-1911.

WALSH, M. J. *Teaching as a Profession.* Henry Holt and Co., New York, 1926.

WHITEHEAD, A. N. *Science and the Modern World.* The Macmillan Co., New York, 1926.